CLARIFICATIONS
ON MASONIC USES

Solange Sudarskis

3

Masonic wanderings

CONTENTS

NB. To save the reader wishing to access documentation references on the web, links with simplified keyboard typing have been created with the *tinyurl.com software* .

1 THE MASONIC TRIPTYCHS

The meaning of initiation

Speculative Freemasonry which was declared initiatory as in this extract from the Revue *Points de vue initiatiques* n°0 of 1958: "Freemasonry is a universal and traditional initiatory order which allows men of good will to participate in the improvement of the human condition, both on the spiritual and intellectual level and on the level of material well-being", or in the principles of the Grand Lodge of France (Freemasonry is a traditional and universal initiatory order based on Fraternity), is today, however, for the Grand Orient, an essentially philanthropic, philosophical and progressive institution, its purpose is the search for truth, the study of morality and the practice of solidarity.

It was recently added: "It attaches fundamental importance to secularism" (article 1 ^{of} its Constitution). As for the DH, its purpose is to "contribute to the moral, intellectual and spiritual development of its members, to promote philosophical and social reflection and to carry out aid, assistance and solidarity operations through purpose-driven associations. non-profit " (art 2

1

of the general regulations of the DH). The contemporary definitions put forward by these Freemasons are ethical and civic , **ignoring a priori any initiatory vision** . In fact, not a word on the initiatory aspect of Freemasonry, this society which, for Mircea ÉLIADE , was the sole beneficiary of the Western initiatory contribution.

For the Ancient duties it was a question of climbing the ladder of the liberal arts as an initiatory ladder which allowed one to know oneself and the world, life in reality, then arriving at the summit of one's arts to see the face of God (knowledge) then go back down to transmit to his Brothers (the word Sister was not yet used due to lack of their presence). In addition to this "liberal" scale, another was essential: that of the cardinal and theological virtues which in all hypotheses offer a return on oneself and others.

And yet, etymology teaches us that the word initiation means "entrance", "beginning". René Guénon himself distinguishes "virtual initiation" from "real initiation", subsequently explaining that "entering the path is virtual initiation", "and following the path is the 'real initiation'; the initiation rites representing the two aspects of the Masonic initiation process. As its name indicates, speculative knowledge is knowledge by reflection while effective initiatory knowledge is direct knowledge, which brings about the identification of the knowing being and the known subject, which is exactly what spiritual realization is.

One is the beginning, the other, the path and the goal.[1]

---

[1] *René Guénon and Masonic initiation* : <tinyurl.com/initiarion-effective>.

All masonry retains the first aspect; it is the goal that differentiates them.

It is not to oppose them to say that initiation, as in the Primordial Tradition (seat of metaphysical knowledge), is the rediscovery of the principles of universal order from which all things proceed, discovery of an experience of an intimate character accompanied by 'a perspective of development, physico-psychological experience, awakening of consciousness, intelligence of the real or the hidden, introduction to the mysteries of life and death, discovery of oneself and others, progress on the path, quest for identity and meaning. It is therefore neither a religious act *stricto sensu* , nor a political meta-narrative, nor a psychoanalysis. The initiatory process develops on an individual, social, intellectual, moral, psychological and spiritual level. Masonic initiation presents some features common to any initiation with its own specificities and variants linked most often to the metaphysical, spiritual, cultural, philosophical and/or psycho-social perspectives in which the seeker situates his quest [2]. The initiatory and mystical elements are

---

[2] Under the name of Royal Art or Sacred Art, the ancient Egyptian priesthoods professed and practiced a whole set of doctrines which have only reached us through a few rare vestiges. These doctrines, as a whole, embraced all the relationships between Man and Nature, and their practice made the initiate King of the Material Universe, hence the Royal Art. Initiation was not a science, because it contained neither rules , scientific principles nor special teaching. It was not a religion since it had neither dogma, nor discipline, nor exclusively religious ritual but it was a school where the arts, sciences, morality, legislation, philosophy and philanthropy were taught, worship and the phenomena of nature, so that the initiate knows the truth about everything.

almost identical, but their dynamics are those, in one case, of a *discipline of interiorization* , in the other case of elevation through the effort of research . *essential* . Thus discursive functions will be put aside in favor of intuitive functions based on analog perception or anagogical vision.

Like its large anthropological family [3], Masonic initiation is an accession to a new "higher" stage, taking place in stages, through particular ceremonies, with reference to a discourse, with a double goal **of socialization and symbolization** . Masonic initiation is therefore at the same time a practice, a development and a corpus, which passes (several times and more or less) through three successive situations:
The nourishment which consisted of the extraction and separation of previous influences, deconstruction; the training which entrusts the elements of the experience of the "knowers", the experience of the myth; the metamorphosis which projects the applicant into a new perception, the transmission of the arcana.

Whatever the case, the journey is always from a status deemed inferior to a status deemed superior, from the outside (profane world, exoteric, conscious environment, "old knowledge") towards the inside (sacred world, esotericism, depth of the psyche, new teachings), symbolically from death to life. Also, if obediences can

---

[3]The structure of the universe in its different planes was known to antediluvian peoples as the laws of Manu (secret code of Atlantis) which influenced Pythagoras and Plato. Herodotus reports that it came from 11,340 before his birth (about 14,000 years before our time).

express themselves when they deem it useful, if the mason as a citizen (and only as such) believes he can "spread to the outside" "truths learned" in the lodge, it is very difficult to do so. initiate to give an account of his own initiation [4].

Tradition is the more or less ritualized continuous transmission of cultural content throughout history from a founding event (real or mythical) or from time immemorial, which constitutes a factor of identity, cohesion and legitimation of a band. Masonic initiation is therefore inherently traditional. Nevertheless, the concepts of primordial tradition, of *Sophia perennis* , universal knowledge of non-human origin theorized among others by René Guénon (1866-1951) or of religious traditionalism legitimizing itself in a revealed tradition, relate to "ideological" choices; various Masonic currents however refer to it explicitly.

If the notion of *origins* allows us to evoke a source, this one necessarily being *pure* , in relation to the subsequent flow of human hazards, the question of transmission , of tradition and its evolution through actualization itself arises.

Masonic initiation

Note that, whatever the rite, the ceremony of awarding a degree is at the same time a practice, a development and a corpus , that is to say a process which appears structured in three phases which,

---

[4] Yves Hivert Messeca, *Masonic initiation between tradition and modernity* : <tinyurl.com/connais-toi-toi-meme >.

normally, should take place in different rooms, even if this is almost never done due to lack of availability of premises.

Thus, except for the first degree singularity, these phases, where the chronological and topological axes are blurred, are :

Phase 1 is located in the space-time of the lodge of the N degree of the Freemason where there is verification of the potentialities of this one, giving viaticum to continue. The Freemason, entered as a candidate, once accepted becomes a recipient.

The transformation of spiritual possibilities from simple potentiality to virtuality must be actualized through initiatory work to allow the abolition of the distance between the subject and the object with a view to a breakthrough towards the absolute. This transmission is a gift/acquisition, the light that the Freemason asks for is given to him; he will receive it if: **he has the potential** ; it is done virtually by **an organization which orders** and develops in a lodge, by means of a rite, symbols as a language for a dawn of words ; he gradually pursues **personal work** through meditation and analogy.[5]

Evolution within the blue lodges supposes three successive levels of meaning. You must first of all **hear** , that is to say, put yourself in a listening situation to record a word, remember an act, print a piece of writing; it is a state of being that requires exercise, training,

---

[5] Analogy according to Aristotle is the resemblance that guides and produces meaning. Similarity is perceived despite the difference, despite the apparent contradiction; it allows us to deploy the vision of a world to liberate it.

discipline. We must then **understand** in order to integrate into ourselves what has been received from the outside; which presupposes, this time, a hermeneutics, that is to say a method of interpretation which allows the deposit received to be translated into an act of being. Finally , we must **transmit** , that is to say make it understandable, not only to ourselves but also to others, the thing received because there is no such thing as a lonely witness, a solitary witness. "Truth begins at two" writes Nietzsche.

Stripping of clothing or stripping of metals are metanoia [6]widely practiced during Masonic ceremonies during this phase. To strip oneself of one's tools for a Freemason is **to free oneself** from the supports which allowed the acquisition of the degree of knowledge which, if it was truly acquired, would then be integrated into one's being. To be able to access a degree of higher order, it would be appropriate for this knowledge of the Freemason **to leave the way clear** again and thereby to get rid of everything which has now become external to the being and which would hinder this next passage, even if these tools have been necessary until then.

Phase 2 is located in the **space-time of the founding myth of grade N+1** . It is developed through its narration to the recipient, and through the experiences of characters from the myth, during alternative role-playing games demonstrating the teaching of the grade. This

---

[6] In ancient Greece, metanoia meant "giving oneself a different, supposedly better, standard of conduct."

epopty [7]conveys the legend of the myth through the incarnation and the trials. The Temple serves as a landmark but also other places such as the crossing of the Jordan, the temple enclosure during Hiram's assassination, the countryside where the search for Hiram's body was carried out, the bridge spanning the Starbuzanai, ... At that moment, there is a phenomenon of assimilation through a psychological identification which is established between the person doing the role-playing and the mythical archetype[8]

It will be noted that in the French Philosophical Rite, during the ceremony of elevation to the 3rd degree, a carpet is rolled out showing the space of the Temple of Solomon. The narration of the murder relates to the orientation of the mythical place, the Temple of Solomon, and not to that of the lugubrious chamber of the lodge.[9]

---

[7] Literary genre of the fantastic short story to give the theatrical representation of myths for the teaching of a secret from stage games.

[8] We speak of Goffmanian interaction. Erving Goffman highlighted the driving role of the relationship at work in interaction. It is neither the structures which determine the actors, nor the actors who generate the structures, but a cognitive relationship which constitutes the engine of a process of subjectivation and socialization. (Céline Bonicco, *Goffman and the order of interaction: an example of comprehensive sociology* : <tinyurl.com/Goffman-interaction>.

[9]Hiram, after visiting the works, directed his steps towards the East Gate where he found the first of the Companions. Hiram sought safety in flight and attempted to escape through the South Gate. The journey always ends in the east of the funeral chamber but it is in the west on the reproduction of the Temple of Solomon which is placed on the ground in the form of a carpet.

Phase 3 is located in the space-time of the lodge at degree N+1 , where the transmission of the arcana of the new degree (the new tools of the initiatory path) is devolved to the recipient to allow him, from these arcana, personal work through meditation. The Freemason has become a neophyte in this new grade. This phase always includes a solemn oath.

Masonic symbolism allows Masons to mean what they think and what they do. The Masonic symbolism is therefore the codified collective representation of Masons. Thus, Masonic initiation is deployed in a specific culture defined as a symbolic system structured around and by language (words, formulas, stories, gestures, sensations, speeches, songs, concepts, myths, etc.) in which each symbol/ sign takes on meaning according to a logic of opposition/sorting/reaction/completeness reducible most often (but not always) to the binary (masculine/feminine, black/white, good/evil, Sun/moon, two columns B. and J.) or in the ternary (triangle/triangulation; sun/moon/venerable; wisdom, strength, beauty; …). Symbolic thinking therefore allows the discovery of areas unexplored by dialectical thinking, by bringing together the opposites.[10]

It is usual in the context of initiation to provide the initiate with a traditional symbolic reference which can only be offered to him; this should not be definitive, but rather as an invitation to travel one's own path, the relevance of which will only become apparent to one later.

---

[10]Yves Hivert- Messeca, *Masonic initiation between tradition and modernity* :: < tinyurl.com/entre-initiation-et-modernite >.

"It is obvious that the **first three degrees of masonry symbolize the life of man** . The first degree takes him from his mother's breast, and takes him until adolescence; the second degree represents it in the age of strength; and finally, the third shows him in old age and leads him to the tomb, from where he seems, in some way, to emerge of himself in the generation that succeeds him [11].

Let us retain some vehicles of initiatory transmission : **symbolism, the Ritual, the Lodge Table, the tests, the founding role of the Venerable, the role of the masters...**

---

[11] Foreword to the *Ritual of the first three degrees according to the ancient notebooks, for the ancient and accepted Scottish Rite* , dated 5829, p.62: <tinyurl.com/Rituel-REAA>.

2 THREE POINTS, THAT'S ALL

Why three points?

In the spiritual arcana, we find the three points in Kabbalah where they are used triangulated, sometimes replacing the tetragram (of the 4 letters, they only retain 3 primordial ones, the letter he appearing twice, the Chaldaic targoum renders it as three yod, ‫יּי‬). In the Hebrew alphabet, the segol is the vowel "é" written with 3 dots (‫א‬ is pronounced [ɛ], like *short).* This structure, which is not a letter, symbolizes by its shape (a triangle whose apex points downwards) the perfect balance of being within universal harmony. The inverted Segol (a triangle whose apex points upwards) is called the Segoltah, it forms with the Segol the *Maghen David* , the star or shield of David, symbol of free trade between our world and the spiritual Worlds .[12]

For Reuchlin, the three points are to be related to the three highest sephiroth of the Tree of life, Kether,

---

[12]Éric Daniel El-Baze, *The Roots of Existence, The Kabbalah of Unveiling* , from p.55: < tinyurl.com/la-kabbale-du-devoilement >.

Hochmah and Binah. Masonic mysticism identifies them with the ternary Wisdom, Strength, Beauty.

However, Albert G. Mackey writes in his *Encyclopedia of Freemasonry* ... **The three dots are not a symbol, but simply an abbreviation mark** . The attempt, therefore, to trace it back to the three Hebrew yods, a Kabbalistic sign of the Tetragrammaton, or any other ancient symbol, is futile. **It is an abbreviation, and nothing more** ; although it is probable that the idea was suggested by the sanctity of the number three as a Masonic number, and **these three points could refer to the position of the three officers of a French lodge** . Ragon says the mark was first used by the Grand Orient de France in a circular dated August 12, 1774, which read "G ∴ O ∴ de France."[13] Why not? But if they are only an abbreviation, then there is a contradiction in Albert Mackey's remarks which also supposes that they would refer to an underlying and therefore symbolic meaning! There is no escaping symbolism in Freemasonry!

The three points arranged in an equilateral triangle, or tripunctuation, are still used today **to identify a signature such as that of a Freemason** , which has earned masons to be called **" three-point brothers "**.

The three points come from the companionship where they seem to have symbolized the triangle. The Companion Union has retained the use of the three points in a triangle, while the Companion Federation

---

[13]Albert G. Mackey , *An encyclopedia of free masonry and its kindred sciences... ,* p. 785: <tinyurl.com/mackey-three-points >.

uses the three points placed at right angles. Finally, the Workers' Association abandoned triple punctuation for a single point after each initial.

The shape of the three points is not always triangular in the signatures of the Freemasons, in particular we note **three points in a line between two lines** in 1760 (the two lines would represent the 2 columns) [14]. However, as early as 1701, in Brest, the bailiff René Le Corre signed with three points in a line between two lines [15].

In 1764, on the 18th [day] of the 3rd [week] of May, in the *Book of Registers* of the respectable lodge of Concorde in the Orient of Beaucaire, tripunctuation already appears to abbreviate words [16]. But the orientation of the triangular shape is not fixed, the top is sometimes directed upwards, sometimes downwards. At the same time, in Italy only two points were used for this purpose [17]. **The shape doesn't matter as long as there are points!**

At the same time as it became one of the elements of the signature, this punctem was fixed in a triangular shape, undoubtedly for symbolic reasons , probably coming from the luminous delta (as we see on Lafayette's signature on the painting of the lodge Les Trois Jours, 1832; note the abbreviation of the word lodge in the form of a rectangle).

---

[14] From page 283 of *Freemasonry in France from the origins to 1815* by Gustave Bord: < tinyurl.com/Gustave-Bord >.

[15] André Kervella, *At the origins of French Freemasonry* , 1889-1750: <tinyurl.com/origines-FM-francaise>.

[16] Book of registers of the respectable lodge of Concorde in the Orient of Beaucaire, p. 5: <tinyurl.com/livre-des-registres>.

[17] Ibid, p. 39.

This figure was introduced into printed matter from 1775 (after having appeared around 1771 and will be generalized from the 19th century) , **to mark an abbreviation of certain words belonging, certainly, to profane vocabulary but which are used in specific way in Freemasonry.**

It is customary, in written exchange, to use, for symbolic words, abbreviations, written with capital letters and followed by three points arranged in a triangle. Initials should be reserved for symbolic words.

To mark the plural, we double the initial letter: Brothers, Sisters: FF ∴ , SS ∴ Thus, the officers appear in the texts as: Vén ∴ (Venerable), Orat ∴ (Speaker), Secr ∴ (secretary), Surv ∴ (Supervisor), Gr ∴ Exp ∴ (Grand expert), M ∴ des Cér ∴ (Master of Ceremonies), Très ∴ (Treasurer), Hosp ∴ (Hospiter), Couv ∴ (Roofer). As a sign of great respect towards the dignitaries, we triple the first letters, example: Very Powerful Grand Commander: TTT ∴ PPP ∴ GGG ∴ CCC ∴

We even find the tripunctuation associated with the abbreviation of the word Lodge (in the form of a rectangle) as on the tomb of Théodore Verhaegen.[18]

In the "Modern Rite of Adoption" the three points are replaced by five points [19].

---

18 *Funeral tribute to Verhaegen* : <tinyurl.com/tombe-Theodore>.

[19] Edmond Mazet, *Notes on the Masonic alphabet* : <tinyurl.com/images-alphabet>.

3 THE ENCRYPTION OF THE MASONIC ALPHABET

There is a Kabbalistic encryption of the Hebrew alphabet called *Aïq Bekar* which uses 9 rooms with one or two points to differentiate each of the 3 letters found in each portion (the letters are placed in order from right to left). Mentioned by Albert G. Mackey in his *Encyclopedia of Freemasonry…*, with the word "cipher", this process is documented by Spartakus FreeMann [20]. This alphabet would have inspired the Masonic alphabet.

The Masonic alphabet is an encrypted alphabet , which replaces each letter to be written by the shape of a portion of the open Saturn square (3 x 3), or of a Saint Andrew's cross in which it is found. This system is reminiscent of Cistercian numbering. It is the geometric shape in a dedicated space that represents its value.

Many variants exist, documented among others, in *Masonic encryption systems* by Philippe Langlet, ed. from The Hut.

---

[20] *The Aïq Bekar or Kabbalah of the Nine Chambers* by Spartakus FreeMann . < tinyurl.com/alphabet-des-neuf-chambres >.

The most likely source seems to be the *Khatam Pharouq or Sceau Rompu* published in 1745: "Maçonne writing combines with the same simplicity the advantage of being a universal writing suitable for all kinds of languages. This wonderful alphabet consists of two parallel perpendicular lines, cut by two horizontal lines also parallel, which forms a regular square in the middle, four open squares and four equal angles. All these divisions form nine boxes, both open and closed. To complete the alphabet we use two lines which intersect in a St Andrew's cross giving 4 boxes. There are several Masonic alphabets which place the letters differently in the 13 boxes (1748, 1791, *original English, improved English, original continental, United states* ....).

This is why it is called the **pigpen** alphabet . The term *pig pen* comes from the way of preparing the symbols used to substitute the letters. In fact, we trace enclosures in which the alphabet is placed. Then simply copy the area corresponding to the desired letter. Thus, to take concrete examples of the current digital Masonic alphabet, the letters a and b are constructed from the top left, truncated box in which they are located. The letter "a" takes the empty box as key; "b" being the following letter, we enter a point in this same box. The "c" will be the next box, a square open upwards, the "d"... We alternate empty box and pointed box; the letter U will have the shape of the left part of the St Andrew's cross, the V will have the shape... of a V.

In writings, **the abbreviation of the word lodges** is the letter L coded in the so-called French alphabet of 1804 (in which the absence of letters j is replaced by i ; k by c; v and w by u), represented by a square (or a rectangle) with, or not, a point in the middle. In the plural, the word "loges" is written with 2 intertwined squares that we find on certain pins.

Often the letters M and B embroidered on master aprons are replaced by their encryption.

By bringing together what is scattered, that is to say the two structures, we obtain a figure containing all the shapes of the letters of our alphabet, as well as our numbers [which have become rounded with use].

Combining the letters with magic squares - such as the one using Agrippa's 5x5 magic square of Mars) - to give their ordinal position in a sentence with a Masonic alphabet - such as the numerical one - makes it possible to encode a mysterious message (without space between the letters). words though).

11	24	7	20	3
4	12	25	8	16
17	5	13	21	9
10	18	1	14	22
23	6	19	2	15

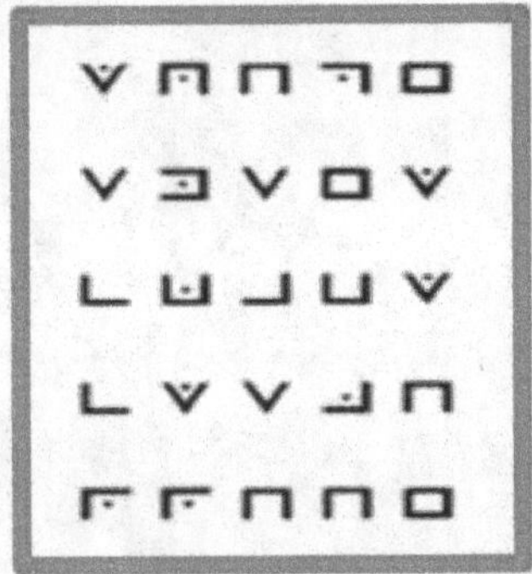

Sois droit et habite ton corps

Some Masonic alphabets

Clarifications on Masonic uses

The hieroglyphs which encrypt letters and numbers vary according to places, times and ranks.

Consult the remarkable research work of Gustave Bord in his book *Freemasonry in France from the origins to 1815* , Volume 1 [21].

---

[21]Gustave Bord, *Freemasonry in France from the origins to 1815* : <tinyurl.com/formes-alphabets>.

4 MASONIC CALENDARS

To make a date is to install a story in a space, it is to find a place for it to be told, for it to be remembered and for us to return to it in order to commemorate it.

On August 9, 1564, by the Edict of Roussillon, King Charles IX imposed January 1 [as] the obligatory starting point of each year, a way of standardizing and bringing order to his kingdom in the midst of a religious war. In 1582, a new calendar was born: the so-called Gregorian calendar, named after Pope Gregory XIII (pope from 1572 to 1582). It is this calendar which is still in force today. But, Great Britain and the Protestant countries only adopted the Gregorian calendar (decreed in 1582) in 1752, preferring, according to the astronomer Johannes Kepler, " *to be at odds with the Sun, rather than in agreement with the Pope* ".

1789, French revolution and revolution in calendars! On September 22, 1792, the Convention proclaimed the Republic. Symbolizing a break with the old order, the start of the new era was set for September 22, 1792, which thus became the 1st Vendémiaire Year I. Each year begins on the day of the autumnal equinox, the moment when the length of the day is equal to that of the night, which, depending on the year, can correspond to September 22, 23 or 24, a date which is fixed by decree. The year is divided into twelve months of thirty days, themselves divided into three " decadi" of ten days (to remove any biblical reference to the seven-day week), followed by five complementary days also called "sans-culottides" . The leap year is called "franciade" and the day is added every four years, Revolution Day. France is the only one to have this calendar! In 1805, a return to the old system became necessary: France must have the same calendar as the rest of Europe. January 1 ' 1806 (11 Nivôse year XIV) thus marks the abandonment of the revolutionary calendar for the Gregorian calendar.

At the REAA, in the blue boxes, we obtain the value of the so-called **true light year** by adding 4000 years to the Christian calendar. It was Reverend Uscher, Anglican prelate of the 16th century [who] gave this date . *Anderson's Constitutions* roughly repeat this dating. It is advisable to use the Julian calendar starting the year on March 1 [(] because it is the month of Aries, 1st [sign] of the Zodiac), for this, we must break down the elements of the date, **we do not use not the names of the current months, only their dates** . Thus, February 11, 2022 vulgar era (*anno domini*) becomes the 11th [day] of the 12th [month] of the year of the True Light 6021; April 18, 2022 is the 18th [day] of the 2nd [month] of the year of True Light 6022 (***anno lucis***).

In fact, Anderson makes the Masonic era begin, not 4000 years ago but 4003 years ago. This is a timeline that relates to the creation of the world. According to this chronology adopted since the 17th [century] , the creation of the world would have taken place in the year 4004 BCE (according to the Irish bishop James Ussher in his work

Chronology dated 1611). Anderson therefore symbolically makes the beginning of Freemasonry coincide with the creation of the non-exclusively Masonic world. The date of " *anno lucis* ", which is affixed to all Masonic documents, is only a philosophical myth, symbolizing the idea which analogically connects the creation of physical light in the universe with the birth of Masonic light or spiritual and intellectual in the candidate.

Over the centuries, there were several established chronologies: 3761 years before the birth of Christ by Jose Ben Halatt, 3952 years by Bede, 4000 years by Isaac Newton .

Generally speaking, French and German lodges use "in the year of the True Light" or the *anno lucis* to symbolically trace the origin of Masonry to the creation of the world according to biblical tradition. The use of Hebrew months is no longer in use today (except sometimes in the Scottish Rite).

This style is not accepted everywhere: Scottish masons use in parallel, especially at the High Grades, at the same time as the Hebrew months, a calendar using Jewish chronology, the **anno hebraico** or the **anno mundi** .

This calendar begins in mid-September and we must add to the Gregorian calendar 3760 years until September or 3761 years later.

The Ancient and Primitive Rite of Memphis Misraïm defines the beginning of the calendar in the year 1292 BCE, which corresponds to the accession to the throne of Ramses II. It is also based on the ancient Egyptian calendar (also called the **Nilotic calendar**) based on the annual fluctuations of the Nile and which had as its primary goal the regulation of agricultural work during the year. We find in this rite that the year begins on August 29 by adding 1291 - corresponding to the coronation of Sethi1 - others propose 1294 year of the construction of the great temple of Abydos and its Osireion. In the Rite of Misraim (official) it begins in the year 1356 BCE, the presumed date of the beginning of the reign of the 9th pharaoh of the 18th dynasty, under the name of Akhenaten. The anniversary of the death of Osiris (many authors see the origin of the myth of Hiram in the death of this god), was celebrated in ancient Egypt on the 17th [day] of the month of Athyr (named after the goddess Hathor).

At the grade of Royal Arch, the date of the starting point of the calendar is that of the beginning of the reconstruction of the Second Temple by Zerubbabel, date fixed at 530 BC. This is the **anno inventionis**. At the rank of *Royal and Select Master*, the starting point is the date of the dedication of the Temple of Solomon, i.e. 1000 BC; this is the **anno depositionis**. In the Templar ranks, we count from the date of creation of the Order of the Temple (1118 AD); it is the **anno ordinis**.[22]

There is a Masonic tradition which precisely locates the **day of Hiram Abif's death**. This date is cited in the rituals of Anglo-Saxon Operative Masonry represented, today, by the Masonic order recognized by the United Grand Lodge of England, *The Worshipful Society of Free Masons, Rough Masons, Wallers, Slaters, Paviors , Plaisterers*

---

[22]Fascinating approach to the *ages of the World* by Jacob Perlman in the magazine *Traditional Renaissance* n° 195-196 from page 260: <tinyurl.com/ages-du-monde>.
Consult the *Masonic Vade-mecum, for the first three degrees of the ancient and accepted Scottish Rite* , starting on page 65: <tinyurl.com/vade-mecum-maconnique> (*download the file for more comfortable access*).

and Bricklayers, or *The Operatives* . In the chapter of the *7th degree* , of the book *Guild Masonry in the Making* (fairly broad overview of the rites and symbols of this operational system) by Charles H. Merz, we can read *1. The Commemoration of the Founding of King Solomon's Temple held in April. 2. The Commemoration of the Death of Hiram Abif,* held **on October 2nd** . *3. The Commemoration of the Dedication of the Temple, held on October 30th* (p. 112).

Blue Lodges Freemason	Anno Lucis 4000 + AD (Anno Domini, current year)	The Craft Masonry calendar begins with the creation of the world and uses the term *Anno Lucis* (AL) – "In the Year of Light." To arrive at this date, they add 4000 to common time (AD), because the Earth was supposed in conventional theology to have begun in 4000 BC.
Royal Arch Masonry Capitalize	Anno Inventionis 530 + AD	The Royal Arch Masons date from the year the second temple was leased by Zerubbabel. *Anno Inventionis* (AI), meaning "in the year of discovery", terminology used by Chapters. This adds 530 to the common time.
Royal & Select Masters Cryptic Masons	Anno Depositionis 1000 + A.D.	The royal and chosen masters or cryptic masons date from the year Solomon's temple was completed. It is called e *Anno Depositionis (* AD), which means "in the year of deposition " and adds 1000 to common time.
Knights Templar	Anno	The Templars begin their timeline with the formation

Clarifications on Masonic uses

Knights	Ordinis AD-1118	of the order in 1118 AD . *Anno Ordinis* (AO), meaning "in the year of the Order." This deducts 1118 from common time.
Ancient and Accepted SCOTTISH Rite	Anno Mundi 3760+AD	Anno Mundi, or the "Year of the World," is analogous to the Jewish calendar (with an extra year added after September). Anno Mundi (AM), meaning "in the year of the world" adds 3760 to common time.
Order of High Priesthood	Anno Benefacionis 1913+AD	Abraham is said to have been blessed by Melchizedek in 1913 BC. J.C.
Holy Royal Arch Knight Templar Priests	Anno Renascent AD-1686	This order is said to have been reestablished in 1686 AD

5 SINGULAR PLURALS

In the Traditions, the plural plays a preponderant role in the number of gifts essential to perform certain rituals : 7 Freemasons make a lodge just and perfect. 10 men (*miniam*) attest to the sufficiency of a group of men of good morals to practice certain prayers, representing a sufficient level of purity. 36 righteous people is the minimum openness of humanity to welcoming the Messiah.

Until about 1726, the regularity of a Lodge depended both on a particular situation and on a qualified quorum. Thus we find, to the question "what is a true perfect Lodge?", different answers in the traditional catechisms of the time (*true prefect lodge*): The statutes of 1670 of the lodge of Aberdeen prescribe that the outfits take place "in the middle of the fields", and that the receptions of apprentices take place "in the old field lodge" in a rural parish in the surrounding area (Miller, Notes *on the early history and records of the Lodge Aberdeen, 1 ter*); a day's walk (travel) from a locality, beyond (the reach of) the bark of a dog or the crowing of a cock (*Manuscript Edinburgh Register House* 1696); on the highest hill or deepest valley in the world, beyond (the reach of) the crowing of a cock or the barking of a dog (*Sloane Manuscript 1700*); on the highest mountains or (in) the deepest valleys of the world (*The Grand Mystery of Free-Masons Discovered 1724*); the center of a true heart (*Graham Manuscript* 1726).

The quorum, for its part, was the required number of masons having various masonic degrees. The differences found in the disclosures take into account a time when there were still only two degrees, then a graduation on the qualifier of the lodge: ***simple, formed or compound; just, composed or governed; perfect or just and perfect.*** Most often as in the RER, RF, REAA: - What do you mean by a just and perfect lodge? - Three form it, five compose it (or enlighten it) and seven make it just and perfect. But we also find: any odd number from 3 to 13 (*Graham*); or 5 companions and 7 apprentices (*A Mason's Confession*).

The *Edinburgh Manuscript* , 1696, in the dialogue of lighting the Fires or consecrating a Lodge practiced by the REAA of the Order of the Royal Secret teaches: "The TIF Grand Orator: For a lodge to be just and perfect, It takes seven Masters, five Apprentices entered, within a day's walk of a town, where one hears neither a dog barking nor a rooster crowing. PWGSC Can't a smaller number make a lodge fair and perfect? The TIF Grand Speaker: Yes, Most Powerful Sovereign Grand Commander: Five Master Masons and three Apprentices entered. PWGSC And even less? The TIF Great Speaker : The more there are, the merrier we are, the fewer guests we have, the better the food !"[23]

---

[23] The manuscript from the Edinburgh archives, 1696, Translated and commented by Edmond Mazet: <tinyurl.com/edimbourgmanuscript>.

However, variations exist on the degrees of each of these groups: what do they consist of? *Trinity College* (1711): Three masters, two journeymen and three apprentices (8 members) *A Masons' Examination* (1723): One master, two proctors, four journeymen, five apprentices (12 members). *The Grand Mystery of Free-Masons Discover'd* (1724): Five or seven upright and perfect Masons (5 or 7 members). *Graham MS* (1726): Any odd number from 3 to 13; the explanation is given: "to the reference to the blessed Trinity, to the coming of Christ with his 12 apostles". *Willkinson MS* (1726): one master, two overseers, two journeymen and two apprentices (7 members). *Masonry Dissected* (1730) and appearance of a structured 3rd Degree: A master, two supervisors, two companions and two apprentices (7 members). It will be noted that with the approach of a 3rd [Degree] since 1724 the number of members to constitute a Just and Perfect Lodge increases to 7 in English masonry. Reported in 1736 in Religious *Ceremonies and Customs of All Peoples of the World* : seven people, namely the master, two inspectors, two brothers and two apprentices form a lodge [24].
French Masonry will use the same ingredients.

The Secret of the Freemasons (1742), The Catechism of the Freemasons (1744), The Order of the Freemasons Betrayed (1745), the Broken Seal (1745), The Desolation of the Modern Contractors of the Temple of Jerusalem (1747)), The New Catechism of Freemasons (1747) indicates: The Grand Master, the first and second Supervisor, two Companions and two Apprentices (7 members). But here

---

[24] < tinyurl.com/parfaite-loge >.

we have the progression 3,5,7 : Three form it, five compose it and seven make it perfect. Same thing with *The precious collection of Adonhiramite Masonry* from 1786 (-What are the three Masons of the simple Lodge ? - One Venerable and two Supervisors. - What are the five of the just? - These are the first three and two Masters. - Finally, what are the seven that make the Lodge perfect? - a Venerable, two Wardens, two Masters, a Companion and an Apprentice).

In the Rectified Scottish Rite we find the same provisions. In the French Rite (1785-1786) which we find in *The Regulator of the Mason* of 1801, similarly, in the REAA, we have: - Three direct it, five enlighten it, seven make it just and perfect. -Explain this answer. - The Three are the V\M\and the two supervisors. These Officers with the Speaker and the Secretary are the five Lights of the Lodge. But at least seven members of the Lodge must be united to be able to carry out regular work. In this new progression 3,5,7, the 5 who enlighten and direct the Lodge are invariably Masters, the other two members are therefore 1 Apprentice and 1 Companion if we follow the logic of the first catechisms. In the *Manual of the Venerable of the first 6 grades* of the Illustrious Order of Strict Observance, p.104, it is written: "9 make it perfect when it has been legally constituted by the Provincial Grand Master and its Venerable has been duly installed".

In conclusion, if there are no Apprentices or Companions on the Columns, the Lodge cannot be opened, even if there are 7 Masters. On the other hand, if there are 5 Masters, 1 Apprentice and 1 Journeyman, the Works can be opened.

We will remember, in the definition of a just and perfect lodge, that the requirement for the presence of seven (7) masons is general [25].

However, if a quota authorizes dressing in a lodge, the isolation through which applicants pass is just as essential in Freemasonry : reflection room, blindfold of darkness, and above all silence of the apprentice. The quest is done both through solitary meditations and through the initiating group. The stages of initiation alternate periods belonging to horizontality (in the search for knowledge and encounters) and periods of verticality where the transformations which result in knowledge take place.

We are aware of coming from elsewhere and of being pursued by this elsewhere which completes all of our references. Initiation, which is an effort upwards, towards the Self, towards a change of state, is not accomplished for everyone at the same pace, but will cause the modification to interfere with the other members of the group. This shows that man is never an individual, he is the core of a whole, that of the past and that of the present. The chain of union, through the weaving of arms and hands, makes us experience achrony in the torrent of the reciprocity of presence, united by an ineffable bond. When the chain is broken , is there only solitude left? In the initiatory journey or the 33 degrees of wisdom, Christian Jacq answers us: "You will be alone, but not isolated like someone who knows nothing other than himself. You will be alone facing the

---

[25] p. 21 , 47 , 77, 103, 134, 154, 160, 166: < tinyurl.com/harry-Carr-catechismes>.

Principle. Alone, while being inhabited by the community of men with whom you travel on the path to initiation.

Symbolism is the instrument par excellence of integration, of breaking with isolation. There can only be solidarity between individuals sharing a symbolic system which makes possible a consensus on the meaning of the world. Symbolism is interpretation by taking from the past what others had already sedimented and embellishing it with the specificity of the intuition of the person who completes it. This search, for what we are at the deepest level of being, the self stripped of the old man and reborn in Oneself, requires others but also solitude; solitude which protects us from all totalitarianisms.

6 GLAIVE OR SWORD?

On a 14th century tapestry [by] Hennequin of Bruges, Jesus Christ appears to Saint John in a vision so extraordinary that the apostle faints at his feet. Christ will need all divine and human weapons to free Christians from the yoke of violence, ignorance and the inclination to sin: hence the sharp sword that he holds in his mouth, symbol of power of the divine word. He is facing, powerful, seated on a throne which shows him in his eternal glory, with the seven candelabra in the background as mentioned in the text of Revelation. " **Do not think that I have come to bring peace on earth: I have not come to bring peace, but a sword.**" This Christ with the double-edged sword symbolizes the intellectual or spiritual tool favoring the transition from the "closed to the open" state.

Sword or gladius? We sometimes find the word sword, sometimes the word sword as for Mathieu; 10.34 (believed to have been written in Hebrew before Greek) " Do not think that I have come to bring peace on earth: I have not come to bring peace, **but a sword** ." Do not think that I have come to bring peace on earth; I did not come to bring peace **but the sword.** This would mean that these two words are synonymous.

However, if we retain as a definition that **"sword"** is an offensive and defensive weapon composed of a long sharp blade and a handle and that the warriors carried at the side in a sheath while **"glaive"** is a sharp and short sword that the Romans used, this is definitely a sword!

We also find this idea with Mañjuśrī, a famous bodhisattva, also considered a tutelary deity of Buddhism. He is represented, in general, with a sword (khadga) of fire symbolizing intelligence in the right hand, and in the left a book/scroll representing transcendent wisdom. With a stroke of his sword, Manjusri is said to have opened the passage to the Baghmati River, drying the valley and allowing access to the Kathmandu sanctuary.

the sword has become an honorary object as a reward for distinction; it was offered to famous gladiators when they were freed.

The name of sword rather than sword finds its explanation in the rank of Knight in this conference: *Sources and history of the rank of Knight Kadosh (Part 1)* .[26]

We see that from 1840, statistically, in the 84 rituals of the kadosh degree studied, the vocabulary used in the rituals of this degree gives preference to the word sword rather than the word sword [27].

---

[26]Video, Round table organized by the Areopagus Research Sources, *Sources and history of the rank of Knight Kadosh (part1)* : < tinyurl.com/chevalier-kadosh >.

[27]Video, Round table organized by the Areopagus Research Sources, *Sources and history of the rank of Knight Kadosh (part2)* : < tinyurl.com/stat-glaive-ou-epee >.

The symbolic sword does not slash in the sense of an irreparable division.

Made of celestial iron, it cuts through imperfections, neutralizes inharmonious mental associations , and allows you to remain coherent in combat. Thus, taking control of it amounts to grasping a ray of light, harmonizing the scattered beams of light, making potentialities grow. The use of the sword would therefore introduce into the consciousness an axis of light, a rectitude essential for experiencing initiation. "The sword that wounds," says Fulcanelli, "the spatula responsible for applying the healing balm , are in truth only one and the same agent endowed with the double power of killing and resuscitating, of mortifying and regenerating, of destroy and organize. Spatula, in Greek, is *spatoula* , σπάτουλα; however, this word is close to the words sword or sword (σπαθί), taking their origin from *spao* (σπάω), to tear off, extirpate, break.

The first swords were short and thick with a blade shaped like a gladiolus, hence the name glaive. The sword would be the attribute of the soldier (destructive warrior weapon) but also that of the legislative, of Justice (symbol of positive power), the sword would be reserved for the knight with the main rite of dubbing. From the reign of Louis XV, all brothers carried the sword on the left side in a sheath. It then symbolized, in a lodge, the social equality of the masons of the time, whether nobles or commoners. But as soon as they returned to the profane world this equality, obviously, ceased.

Today, it is worn collectively in lodges in the Rectified Scottish Rite. Out of its sheath, point low in rest position or otherwise on order of the Venerable Master, it is held in the hand by all the masons working on this rite. It is also with the left hand that the Venerable Master, when he sits in the East, holds his sword pointing upwards.

For other rites, only two things remain from the past: a rosette at the end of the master's baldric, a souvenir of the entry into the scabbard, and a sword at the disposal of the masons of the columns near their seat. In rituals after 1843, it is most often called a sword.

The sword, held by the members , is at the same time:
~a weapon whose clanks, when they collide, symbolize the fight of men to conquer and triumph over their passions, -
~a transmission of the beneficial energy of all the members of the Lodge to the applicant at the moment when the blindfold is removed during his initiation
~a warning of the punishment which would threaten perjury,
~an honor paid to visiting dignitaries by forming, for their passage, the steel vault.

The sword is always held in the left hand by the freemason of the order, except by the roofer and the experts who hold it in the right hand.

The roofer's sword is an instrument which prohibits access to the temple to the uninitiated; from this role of guardian of a sacred place, it derives its function of protecting the temple internally and externally.

The expert's sword is the symbol of respect for values: it is the guardian of the ritual and the actor in its implementation. It is the moral and spiritual weapon of the mason reminding him of his duties and obligations.

The flaming sword , wielded by the Venerable, placed in the East on its board, dominates the other swords. It is made of a pointed steel blade with two edges, attached to a handle equipped with a guard, this sword with a sinusoidal blade represents the symbol of the initiatory power of the venerable. It is used during initiations, passages or elevations.

The word translated from Hebrew, which describes the **blade of the flaming sword** is the verb " **to turn, to change** ". It is therefore a sword which is always turning, which is moving, hence its flamboyant character. Indeed, this Hebrew root also shows that the sword blazes because it is fire itself and because it reflects solar light. The double edge of the blade has a double function: that of carrying the fire of creation to give life to the initiate, that also of deciding between several possible choices when the life of the Lodge is involved.

Weapon of Light , the flaming sword is related to lightning, lightning. This fiery weapon symbolizes the fight for the conquest of Knowledge by cutting through the darkness of ignorance.

It is also the representation of the Sun by the brilliant ray of its wavy blade; we can then speak of a **flaming sword** . This Light is a connection with the Great Mysteries: through ritual thought, it kills, in the applicant, the non-initiable part so that a new life is born in him through access to vision and understanding. , beyond the appearences.

The flaming sword is that of the cherub who dispenses life and death, who sweeps away pride, who dissolves the ego. She guards the door to the other world, that of the source of Light. To enter this world, you must pass through the edge of this sword. With his flaming sword, the Venerable shows his function as guardian of the symbol, that of the regeneration of Man through the work of dissolution of the self, of the birth of light in pain, the immutable and necessary law of initiations and tests.

When the venerable places the flaming sword on the head of the novice, pronouncing the ritual words, "I create you, constitute and receive a freemason", the light, then dispensed, is a double energy: creative and protective fire which installs the new mystery in the cosmos of the lodge. It is at this moment that the recipient becomes a neophyte. This is in analogy with the lightning of the creation of the Sephiroth tree.
The Flamboyant Sword is precisely there to remind us that it is the function and the edictive word of the venerable that transmits, not any individual.

At the 7th degree of the REAA, we no longer speak of a sword, but **of a saber** and in the three following degrees, **of dagger** . For example, in the 10th century swords became daggers, recalling the name of the jewel worn at these degrees: a golden dagger with a silver blade, suspended at the bottom of the cord . At the 11th degree, the dagger takes the name "sword of Justice" completing the ranks of vengeance.[28]

In chivalric rites , throughout the duration of the outfit, the handling of the sword is extremely codified and it

---

[28]Ritual of the 10th degree REAA – Illustrious Elect of the Fifteen: < tinyurl.com/the-poignard >.

must, under no circumstances, be taken out of its sheath without reason; here is an example.

Swordsmanship in the Order of the Temple[29]

Since the handling of the sword must be executed as below, this gesture is very "militarized". Carried out synchronously by the brothers, there is no doubt, it must create a body of unanimity.

Draw

1-Grasp the sheath with your left hand. At the same time, quickly pass your right hand in front of your chest and grasp the hilt of the sword. Extend the blade until the forearm is horizontal across the chest, while firmly holding the sheath with the left hand.

2- Gently withdraw the sword until the tip is free from the sheath, then quickly bring it to the "Present"! While bringing the left hand to the side.

3- Lower the sword to the "Porter"! When the Marshal does not have to draw his sword and we cannot therefore settle on him, we will settle on the Chev\ of the southern column closest to the east.

To present

Hold the blade vertical, the back of the hand forward, the elbow to the body, the cruciform hilt of the sword at the height of the mouth, approximately 3 centimeters. It is not appropriate to kiss the hilt or touch it with your lips when you are in this position.

---

[29] The full name of this order is: *The United Religious, Military and Masonic Orders of the Temple and Saint John of Jerusalem, Palestine, Rhodes and Malta* .

To carry
Hold the forearm horizontal, the hand at elbow height, the elbow glued to the body, the blade vertical, the cross of the guard resting in the hollow located between the thumb and the first knuckle of the index finger (you can leave the little finger of the right hand behind the hilt of the sword).

Rest
1. Move the left foot approximately 30 centimeters to the left.
2. Let the sword fall on the shoulder, halfway between the neck and the end of the right shoulder, slightly loosening the fingers.

Sheath
L. Bring the sword to the "Present"!
2. Grasp, with the last three fingers of the left hand, the sheath below the opening, leaving the thumb and index finger free. Slide the tip of the sword into the opening of the sheath, guiding it with the thumb and index finger of the left hand (do not follow with your eyes, the movement is much easier to perform without looking). Lower the sword into the sheath until the right forearm is horizontal across the chest.
3. Quickly slide the sword into the sheath, if possible in sync with the other knights, then bring the hands to the sides.

To order

"Knights, my Brothers!"

1. Everyone gets up and stands up straight or straightens up if they are already standing.

"To order!"

2. Bring the sword to position 1 of "Draw" and look at the Camp Marshal or Knight closest to the east, south side.
3. Draw the sword and come to the "Present".
4. Lower the sword to the "Porter".

To take place

"Knights, my Brothers!"

Look at the Marshal of Camp or the Knight closest to the east, on the *south side*.

"Take place!"

1. Sheath *position 1*.
2.Resheath *position 2*.
3.Resheath *position 3*.
4. *Sit down.*

Engage

"Engage!" (starting from "Porter")

1. Bring the sword to the "Present".
2. Raise the right arm in maximum extension, 45 ° in front of you, the sword in the extension of the arm, and engage the blade with that of the Knight face to face, edge to edge.

" Carry!" (starting from "Engage")

1. Bring the sword to the "Present".

2. Lower the sword to the "Porter".

Return

"Return your swords!" (starting from "Porter").

1. Tilt the blade to the left until it is horizontal, grasp the blade in the middle with your left hand.
2. Continue to rotate the blade until vertical, in line with the middle of the body, with the guard upwards. Drop your right hand to your side.
3. Tilt your head forward, keeping your eyes focused on the hilt of the sword.

"Carry your Swords!" (starting from "Return")

1. Raise your head.
2. Rotate the sword to the right, until it is horizontal; then grab the hilt with your right hand.
3. Bring the sword back to the "Porter" then let the left hand fall to the side.

Handing over the sword
When the sword is presented to a knight of higher rank (for example by the Marshal de Camp to the Eminent Preceptor or by an officer to the Eminent Preceptor during the investiture), it is presented on the forearm left, the handle turned towards the senior officer.
When the sword is returned to a knight of lower rank (for example by the Eminent Preceptor to the Marshal of Camp or to an officer during his investiture, the sword is held vertically, by the hilt, between the thumb and the index finger of the right hand, then placed in the right hand of the knight.

You will find the question of the relationship of the sword and the ban on iron in the booklet *ON Masonic decorations* in the chapter *Leave metals at the door of the temple.*

Clarifications on Masonic uses

7 IT'S GOING TO BE GREAT!

The headgear, as its name suggests, is a head adornment to which traditions give meaning.

In the East, generally speaking, the hairstyle was once considered to symbolize the honor and dignity of the wearer; we willingly swore by it; harming it was considered a particularly serious insult. The head is the summary of the body. What is placed on the head, the headgear, has the value of accomplishment and must be in concordance in nature with the person who wears it, therefore depends on the state of consciousness reached.

Let us recall, for example, that the Egyptian gods have their heads covered with a symbol, that the Greek priests crowned themselves when they offered a sacrifice, that Nicolas Flamel wore a cap and that in fact, all the alchemists represented in the Middle Ages WORE a hat of various shapes.

If we refer to the Bible , the high priest wore a head covering. It was not until around the 2nd [century] CE that the wearing of hats began to be extended to all Jews following a Talmudic discussion about respecting and fearing God.

When in the Middle Ages this custom was adopted, it was considered that everyone was similar to the high priest and , at the same time, it was affirmed that the hat recalled that there is always something between man and God. The Talmud teaches that wearing a yarmulke (or having one's head covered) is intended to serve as a reminder that God is the Supreme Authority above all. The Yiddish word for headgear, *yarmulke* , comes from the Aramaic *yira malka* which means "fear of the King". In Hebrew, the head covering is called Kippah, literally "dome".

The hat is also the substitute for the crown , a symbol of royalty, both temporal and spiritual. The man who wears a crown can therefore be considered as the one who joins the earth to the sky, and reciprocally he conducts the influx coming from the sky towards the earth. In this sense the man who wears the hat is a standing man, an *axis mundi* , his mind and gaze stretched towards the sky. "I crown you above yourself" Virgil said to Dante before leaving him. Thus crowned, he joins Béatrice who takes him to paradise.
A French Freemason from the time of Chevalier Ramsay is represented with a **tricorn hat** .[30]

Napoleon will only wear a bicorne made of beaver felt, most often in battle.[31]

---

[30]*Initiatory Points of View* magazine n° 31-32, p 73.

Symbol of the polytechnician's full uniform, the wearing of the **cocked hat** falls under the regulations: "the hat leaves the left part of the forehead exposed, touches the right ear and divides the right eyebrow into medium and extreme proportions." In short , a way to inscribe the divine proportion on your forehead!

The Regulator of Masons of 1802 mentions for the Grade of Master: "Le F .·. The Preparer will take care to have the Aspirant's hat and sword given to the T .· .R.·." (p.8) "All the Brothers will be dressed in black with their hats on their heads and pulled down". In this Ritual, we return the new Master his sword, then his hat, adding " from now on you will be covered in the Master's Lodge, this very ancient custom announces freedom and superiority" (p.26).[32]

Today, in certain rites, the masters must wear a head covering (hat, cap). In the Operative Rite of Solomon (ROS), upon elevation to Mastery, the Expert dresses the new Master in the *decorations of the degree* : the apron, the scarf and the **head covering** .
The ritual of the third degree REAA of the GLDF specifies that "in the Middle Chamber all the Masters wear their hat"

---

[31] This does not mean in battle, but the hat worn with the horns (points) parallel to the shoulders. His hats were all made by the hat maker Poupard: <tinyurl.com/bicorne-de-bonaparte>.
[32] *The Regulator of the mason, 3rd grade* , 1802: <tinyurl.com/Regulateur-du-macon >.

At the RER, if the rite is very traditionally respected, all the masters of the lodge should be covered. "May it be on your forehead the symbol of the spirit of justice, temperance and prudence which must accompany masters in all their endeavors. From now on, you will be able to always cover yourself with it in the lodge, in order to announce the superiority that this rank gives you over apprentices and companions. When they speak, the brothers, except the Venerable and the Supervisors, uncover themselves and if the venerable takes off his hat to receive a brother, all those present must do the same. Since the 18th century, their hat has been a black tricorn bordered with gold braid whose round cap is a symbol of the sky (the Quakers of Amsterdam in the 18th century wore similar ones) [33].

At the French Rite Groussier, wearing a hat has fallen into disuse. It is the same REAA, even if, in the 1st degree of Scottishism, the Venerable is covered only at the opening and closing of the works. In the Emulation Rite, the wearing of a hat is prohibited although certain old English documents indicate that the master of the lodge had to be covered, signifying his role and status, like the crown of King Solomon. RY. If traditionally observed, the Worshipful Master wears a top hat or "clack".

In the 19th century 'adopted Masonry sisters rarely wore hats. It must also be said that their very elaborate hairstyle looked like fascinators. [34]

---

33 Religious *ceremonies and customs of all the peoples of the world,* p.202: < tinyurl.com/coutumes-du-monde>.
34 Gouache painting (early 19th century): <tinyurl.com/chapeau-feminin >.

In the 20th century ' Parisian dressing rooms with a strong female presence were sometimes places for exhibiting eccentric creations by milliners. Today they have adopted, more soberly, the cap, with the same use and the same symbolism as the brothers' hat.

We can understand that the hat, as a symbol of man's limits - like "know thyself" - shows him his capacity for humility in the face of mystery.

Clarifications on Masonic uses

8 THE CHAIN OF UNION, A FRATERNAL STASIS

In most rites, at the end of each outfit, the brothers (and sisters) form a chain by holding each other's ungloved hands; this chain extends to all humanity. The Chain of Union particularly symbolizes the fraternity which unites the Freemason on the one hand with all living Freemasons, on the other hand with all those who preceded him and all those who will succeed him. It should be noted that the unlimited Chain of Union towards the future appears to have, in the past, no other delimitation than the point which would correspond to the very origin of the human species. It places each participant in the continuity of Tradition.

A little historical memories

The first Masonic description of the chain of union seems to appear in 1696 in these lines from the *Edinburgh Manuscript* which alludes to the transmission of secret words: Then all the masons present whisper to each other the word, starting with the youngest, until it reaches the master mason, who gives the word to the entered apprentice.

In the lodge, we find in the ritual of the Scottish Lodge of Bordeaux (1750), the Chain of Union at the close of work at the rank of Perfect Elected Master, or Grand Scotsman (tenth and last grade) then at the close of the first degree of the ritual of the Scottish Mother Lodge of Avignon of 1774.

The Chain of Union appeared in 1766 in the Adhoniramite rite at the end of table work.

On the RER, the Chain of Union appears, as practiced today at the closing of the 1st degree Works [in] the ritual adopted in 1782 in Wilhelmsbad: the brothers form the chain, arms crossed, around the Lodge board. First the Venerable passes the annual message of the previous year then that of the current year and then he says a prayer before breaking the chain and completing the closing of the work.

In the ritual of 1785, adopted by the GODF (at the origin of the *Regulator*), the circulation of the kiss was systematic at the close of the banquets which always followed the outfits: the Venerable gives it to his neighbor on the right, and it returns to him to the left. However, a chain was formed during the seventh and final health, during the Song of the Entered Apprentice. It was the same in *The Order of the Freemasons Betrayed* (1745) or in *The Three Distinct Blows* (1760).

" At the GODF, all Masons who, following a general verification, were recognized as regular, received communication, from 1777, of a double word of recognition, renewed every six months. This measure has remained particular to French Masonry, the use of semester words not having spread [35]abroad, where "tiling" continues to be carried out on all its former scale .

In the Amiable ritual of 1887, a short Chain of Union will be made for the transmission of the semester words.

The Semester Words, specific to each obedience, are communicated twice a year, sometimes only once, during a Chain of Union by the Venerable to the members of the Lodge. These are two words used to recognize active Freemasons. Their knowledge makes it possible to verify the Masonic assiduity of those who present themselves at the entrance of a lodge that they are visiting. The list of the different semester words is communicated to the Roofers of the different lodges of "friendly" obediences. Their ignorance and non-communication by an unknown visitor could prove to the Workshop a prohibited intrusion.

According to Jules Boucher, it is forbidden to write them down and communicate them to anyone who has forgotten them; only the Venerable can transmit them.

The transmission of the two semester words, generally the name of a character linked to Masonry and a virtuous quality beginning with the same initial, is done by whispering ; the first word circulates on the South side,

---

[35]Oswald Wirth, *The Apprentice's Book* in the chapter The Grand Orient of France: <academia.edu/28791571/>.

the second, on the North side. During a Chain of Union, the Venerable transmits a word to his right to the 1st ^{Supervisor} as discreetly as possible. The one who receives it in turn transmits it to the one linked to him on his right. The word thus circulates until returning to the Venerable. The latter at the same time transmits to his left to the Second Supervisor the second word which circulates in the other direction to return to the Venerable who announces that the words have returned "just and perfect". How many transformations these words made us smile when they returned to the ear of the Venerable; incomprehension and ignorance (of the link which cannot recognize what it hears) propagate cumulative approximations of words and what about the ROPM which communicates semester words, in addition to French, sometimes in Hebrew, sometimes names of pharaohs!

At the REAA, in 1923, a Chain of Union was made to receive the recipient of the first degree, and it will be integrated, on an optional basis, at the end of the work in 1962 with the following clarification: we leave the chain "after having shaken arms three times.

Each mason present constitutes a link . Union is generally represented by five symbols: the chain, the knot, the entwined hands and the ring.

In a short chain, Freemasons cross their arms in front of them and take the supinated left hand of their left neighbor (to receive) with their pronated right hand (to give back what has been received). Ideally, it is practiced with arms and legs apart, feet in contact; each Freemason is then a pentagonal star connected to the others – all forming a constellation. These stars come to life when the arms are raised three times to the injunction : " *Let's leave this chain!* » In a long chain, we take the right hand of the neighbor on the left in the left hand. In this form, the chain of union is absent from the English Emulation Style Rite.

Holding hands is not enough to fluidize the energy that must flow and pass through everyone in the closed circle. What is received must be returned to the knot of the hands, recalling those of the lakes of love of the Serrated Tuft which constitute the symbol. "The iod hand that gives, the kaph hand that receives [36]."

In magic, as in magnetotherapy, the left hand sucks the energy (supinating the forearm, the palm turned towards you), it is supposed to receive it; while the right hand dispenses it by returning the gift (in pronation, the palm of the hand turned away from the face). Each individual can always recharge according to their own rhythm, as long as they know how to connect to a source, whether within themselves or outside their physical body. In the Chain of Union, the mason is like a battery with its polarities. The closed circle — with the Freemasons placed in series between their sisters and brothers — creates a magnetic field in the center of the lodge where each balances their energy with that of all the participants by tuning, not by gesture, *but* by *this* gesture, this gesture made in this way, with this ardor, this desire, this application... this respect. The swing of the arms allows, at the end of the chain, to gently cut off this flow, which, too quickly, could give off an electromagnetic discharge.

---

[36]Frank Lalou: <tinyurl.com/la-chair-des-lettres>.

In doing so, the circle thus formed by the members can symbolize the universal brotherhood of Masons in which each initiate is a link in the chain; this multiplication of rings can symbolize "the preservation of unity through multiplicity". It is the inscription of the Freemason in the "Great Time", that of the living, the dead and those not yet born. This cosmic time is also symbolized by the string. The chain of union symbolizes on the microsmic and human level what the cord with its lakes of love (the serrated tassel) symbolizes on the macrocosmic level, order and universal harmony [37].

For Bruno Étienne, "the fusion between all beings makes them participate in the totality of energy by bringing together the micro and the macro" (*A path for the West: Freemasonry to come* , Dervy, 2012). It is a change of state of being, which can last a few seconds, where we feel very good. The moment this happens, there is no more time, only real joy. There is no longer an exterior or an interior. **There is no more me, only a vibrant, luminous I, without gravity or duration, a pure fraternal Being in an ecstasy/enstasy.**

According to scientific studies, the human heart generates the strongest magnetic field in the body, but data transmitted by satellites has been able to demonstrate that the Earth's magnetic field is modified by the emotional changes experienced by its population. By analogy, we find an interesting idea when reading the book by the late astrophysicist Hubert Reeves: " *Patience in the Azure* ". We will remember from his chapter on

---

[37] René Guénon: <tinyurl.com/symbole-science-sacree>.

energies that the mass of the bodies studied, whatever their dimensions, taken in isolation, weighs more than the mass of these same bodies connected in a common structure. For example, the sum of the masses of an electron and a proton is greater than that of a hydrogen atom which they constitute by combining. The difference in weight is due to the emission of an ultraviolet photon, released when an atom is formed. Likewise, a proton and a neutron weigh more separately than combined into a deuteron nucleus. By combining, the two particles release energy in the form of a gamma ray. We call force what allows elements to bind together in constituted bodies: electromagnetic force for atoms, nuclear force for nuclei, Quarkian for nucleons, gravitational for the stars: *May force support our work*. The force of the maç ritual combines our individual spirits to form the egregore particularly felt during the chain of union. So, let's make a hypothesis: as it forms, the egregore releases energy which manifests itself elsewhere. When we become stones of the temple, the transmutations of 2 produce the 3-which-is-one and release energy. Thus "egregorization" releases an energetic who-ne-knows-what that is very difficult to characterize with precision. But, this who-ne-knows-what, in the elsewhere where it is projected, is a radiance whose influence could be the exhalation of our fraternal ritual ceremonies, protected by wisdom and beauty, joy, peace, harmony and love, going to deliver their forces in a battle of energies of good against those of evil.

Some approaches to the notion of egregore

According to Greek etymology: " *egregorein* / *egregoros* " to watch / watchman egregore has two meanings. **It is on**

the one hand the name of angels present on Mount Hermon who united with the daughters of Seth, in Jewish legends, on the other hand an esoteric concept whose approximate definition is that of a "to be collective".

In the Esoteric Doctrines, the mysterious symptoms linked to the psychic entities found in the Groups have been largely associated with the ancient occult idea of an Egregor, and with Egregoric Manifestations.

The word first appears in the Ethiopian and Hebrew book of Enoch, there it designates a category of angel. According to this book: the *Égrègora* , awakener, awakener, watcher are a particular angelic order. Tradition says that some of them rebelled against God, then with one accord they came down to earth and seduced the daughters of men, teaching them many things, from metallurgy to astronomy and astrology, sciences linked to natural laws, and not to Divine Law.

Then it will be Eliphas Levi who will use the term in his book *Dogme et ritual de la haute-magique* , and will give it a Latin etymology instead of Greek, which will cause confusion in its definition (*Eliphas Levi uses "egregore" for egregore*. The word "eggregore" is composed of the two Latin words *Eggregius* and *gregorius* , it means an eminent and collective excellence. The Eggregore, according to the very meaning of their name, would be, for him, compounds of various powers united). René Guénon the critic considering that he gave it an improbable Latin etymology, making it derive from grex, flock", whereas this word is purely Greek and has never meant anything other than "watchman" (Fred Mc Parthy, *What is or is not an egregore* : <omra-fm.fr/ce-quest-ou-nest-pas-un-egregore/>).

The disciples of Martinès de Pasqually designated the invisible Collective of the Order under the name "egregore", and generally any principle of occult manifestations.

According to Robert Ambelain, the name egregore is given to a force generated by a powerful spiritual current and then fed at regular intervals, according to a rhythm in harmony with the universal Life of the Cosmos, or to a meeting of entities united by a character common. In the invisible, outside the physical perception of man, artificial beings exist, generated by devotion, enthusiasm, even fanaticism, which we call egregores.

Daniel Ligou, in his *Universal Dictionary of Freemasonry,* defined egregore as follows: "term used by symbolists to designate the force of cohesion in a human group; in Freemasonry, a Lodge.

It is to the doctor Pierre Mabille, a fellow traveler of surrealism, that we owe another definition of the term egregore in his work *Egrégores ou la vie des civilizations* , published in 1938: "I call egregore, a word formerly used by hermeticists, the human group endowed with a personality different from that of the individuals who form it. Although studies on this subject have always been either confused or kept secret, I believe it is possible to know the circumstances necessary for their formation. I immediately indicate that the essential condition, although insufficient, lies in a powerful emotional shock. To use chemical vocabulary, I say that synthesis requires intense energetic action. The egregore is a living entity, a vitalized concept, a real entity, which to be viable, must be regularly nourished by the members of the group all maintaining the same vibrational energy. The egregore has both a psychic and energetic component. It is an energy which contains all the vibrations of the people who create it, bring it to life... The concentration of people gathered for the same goal, with the same intense thoughts creates an egregore which is constituted, develops, amplifies and becomes active. An egregore can be perceived as the vibrational resonance emitted by the psyche of a group of people vibrating on a specific note. The actions, emotions, thoughts and ideals of each entity constituting this group merge to build a coherent whole, a form whose components are energetic in nature. The notion of egregore is close to that of the collective unconscious, collective consciousness, morphogenetic field or field of consciousness operating between them.

It could turn out that when several people unite around an idea, or a principle, they give birth to an intelligent collective being, which will subsequently become independent, leading a life of its own. It would then be the sum of the psychic energies emitted by each of the members having participated in its emergence, or even in its multiplication. All of these vibratory movements could exert, in return, by virtue of the action-reaction principle, a powerful influence on the components of the group, which can be very different from the psyche of each individual. The total would not be the sum of the component members....

Carl Gustav Jung, with his work on symbols, on myths, on the unconscious, on depth psychology, arrived at the notion of a collective unconscious. A sort of cultural heritage of our ancestors, a sort of summary of the inner experiences of Humans.

An egregore can, however, be disturbed by the negative thinking of people who are not in agreement with the goals. Therefore, esoteric groups try to protect themselves from negative thoughts that could affect their egregore.

Extend with article *The effect of masonic ritual* by Kristine Wilson-Slack (in English).[38]

The formation of the Chain

In the French Rite and the REAA, in the Chain of Union, the Worshipful Master and the Grand Expert are always facing each other in the axis of the lodge – the Worshipful Master, east side; the Grand Expert, west side. The two Supervisors supervise the Grand Expert. All other members present are distributed indiscriminately in the chain. During an affiliation or reinstatement, the affiliated or reinstated Freemason is placed between the Grand Expert and the First Supervisor. During a reception ceremony, each new apprentice is supervised by two participants in the work.

---

[38] *The effect of masonic ritual* by Kristine Wilson-Slack: <tinyurl.com/agence-rituel-maconnique>.

In the Emulation Style Rite, the Chain of Union is not materialized by taking the hands. It resides, in fact, at the opening as well as at the closing of the work in the words: "Unite with me to open the lodge…" and "Unite with me to close the lodge…"

In the RY, the Chain of Union only appears from the degree of Royal Arch Mason (first category of High Grades) and with a different connotation (in Scotland, this grade is still practiced according to its origin, in blue lodge and in addition to the rank of companion).

The Chain of Union can be formed, outside of the outfits, in special circumstances of a banquet, a funeral.

For a detailed approach to the main elements of the chain of union : the cosmic symbol of the chain of union, the circle formed by the chain, necessarily closed, the polarity, highlighted by the crossing of the arms, the hand which plays an active role in the formation of the chain, refer to the text by Robert Mingam, *The Union Chain.*

Text of the Chain of Union, adopted in 1992 by the GODF and given during the Lighting Ceremony of a Workshop.

The Worshipful Master - Let us never forget that fraternal love, as the so-called Anderson Constitutions of 1723 teach us, is the basis, the cornerstone, the cement and the glory of our old brotherhood. Of all our Rites, let us venerate the one whose mission is to constantly remind us of the bond that unites us. May our hearts come together at the same time as our hands, may brotherly love unite all the rings of this chain freely formed by us. Let us understand the beauty and grandeur of this symbol, let us be inspired by its deep meaning. This chain binds us in time as in space, it comes to us from the past and tends towards the future. Through it we are linked to the lineage of our ancestors, our venerated Masters who formed it yesterday, through it the Freemasons of all Rites, of all countries, must unite. Let us enrich it with numerous and solid rings of pure metal and, raising our minds towards the ideal of our Order, let us strive to bring all men together through fraternity. My Brothers, let us extend our right hand forward and promise to maintain, towards one another, the most fraternal affection and to work tirelessly for the realization of Universal fraternity. The Brother Great Expert - In the name of all the Brothers present in this Temple, I promise.The Venerable Master- I take note of your promise ; my Brothers, let us leave the Channel. Our hearts will remain united.

By mixing our breaths in a closed space, we breathe, like a chain of union, the particles of our being-together which transform the self into Us.

It is with the mischievous look of our TCF Fouqueray that we can wonder if, by speculation, we are only dreaming of an idealized chain of union [39].

However, the chain of union is like a heart, a particular place for there to be life where receptivity and activity are combined into each other through what receives and gives.

---

[39] Video: <tinyurl.com/Franck-Fouqueray>.

By its similarity with the Chain of Union, it is appropriate to evoke the chain of alliance [40]made during the ritual ceremony of the operative companions. Wearing their colors, the companions hold hands while crossing their arms like the links of a chain and form a closed circle, rotating in the direction of the movement of the sun, a circle in the middle of which are three companions or two companions and the Mother [41], these remaining motionless. The Rouleur sings the Sons of the Virgin, the refrain of which is taken up in chorus. During the funeral, the Chain is held without singing, it is open, thus symbolizing the link which has just broken.

---

[40] *The Ritual of the Chain* , par. 16: <tinyurl.com/chaine-d-alliance>.

[41]The cayenne, seat of a society of Companions, is a term used among carpenters, roofers, bakers while others, such as carpenters, use the word room. This house is managed by a woman: "Lady Bursar", "Lady Hostess" or "Mother" depending on the degree of initiation received by the latter, both innkeeper and supervisor of morals; her husband takes the name "Father". The Rouleur, or Rôleur, traveling companion was formerly responsible for hiring, now he assists the director, while often acting as Master of Ceremonies.

9 DRINK FROM THE CUP OF BITTERNESS

During the first grade tests, a beverage is drunk by the applicant from a cup called "bitterness" or "cup of libations" [42]; the taste emotion creates a sensory shock which will transform into a lasting memory.

The strict rituals of the RÉAA only provide for two cups, the cup of libations, tasteless then bitter (with a little aloe), which is presented before the first journey at the time of the oath. It is the symbol of the bitterness and remorse that would be left in the recipient's heart by the perjury that had stained his lips, if he broke his solemnly given word to remain silent about the trials he will undergo. Thus, we find, in the *Notebook of Rituals of the three symbolic degrees of the ancient-accepted Scottish Rite* , the details of the posture and the verbal content of the oath of the rituals practiced in the [19th] Century [43].

---

[42] The term "libation" refers to the vocabulary of ancient sacrificial rites: it designates the action of pouring a liquid (wine, oil, milk) as an offering to a divinity, on the ground or on an altar.
[43] p. 51: <tinyurl.com/cahier-des-rituels>.

At the RÉAA, practiced in particular at the DH, during the first degree initiation ceremony, the recipient, still under the blindfold, drinks successively from three different cups into which a beverage has been poured which, from sweet at first, becomes very bitter , then becomes even softer again. By analogy, the bitter drink recalls the difficulty presented by the path of virtue; the initiate must show that by overcoming his disgust his perseverance in the effort will allow him to find the serenity of the adept. This cup is emblematic: the bitterness of this drink symbolizes the difficulty we have in quitting the bad habits we have contracted. As reported by J.-é. Marconis de Négre in *The Golden Bough of Eleusis* [44]: " Follow with courage the path of virtue, and never let yourself be put off by the annoyances that passions may throw at you."

---

[44] Whose full title is: *The Golden Bough of Eleusis, containing: The Abridged History of Masonry, its origin, its mysteries, its civilizing action, its goal and its introduction into the various countries of the world; the origin of all rites and the names of their founders; the table of all the Grand Lodges, the place where they are established, the year of their foundation; the rite they profess, the name of all the great masters who govern them; the number of those covered by it; the ninety-five Rituals of Masonry, containing all the knowledge of the most universally practiced rites, the explanation of all the symbols, emblems, allegories, hieroglyphs, characteristic signs of all degrees, and the Perpetual Calendar of all Masonic rites; the Templar Kadosh with the agape of the former initiates; the Grand Chapter of the Knights of the Growing Rose; the Universal Tiler; the five Rituals of Masonry of adoption for ladies, with the complete Tiler, etc.* (p.86): <tinyurl.com/rameau-dor-dEleusis>.

The cup presented in the Operative Rite of Solomon is called the "sacred cup". At the Rite of Memphis-Misraïm, a first cup is offered to the blindfolded applicant who has just passed through the lower door and before making him make the three journeys. It is the Brew of Oblivion (recommended by the ritual: a cold infusion of hawthorn): " this brew aims to depersonalize you. A few weeks after its ingestion is harmless to physical health, your past personality will slowly dissolve. Insensibly, with the days, you will become another being. Slowly but surely, the egregore who animates and leads our ancient Society will penetrate you, will substitute his will for yours and, on the next anniversary of your Reception, there will be nothing left of the man (woman) that you currently are . . Then a second cup is presented to the neophyte just before he takes his oath, which he drinks in three installments. It is a bitter beverage (recommended by the ritual: an infusion of gentian), that of memory, the water of Mnemosyne. " Earlier, you drank the Brew of Oblivion, intended to depersonalize you, to remove all your will. Here is a second cup, that of the Drink of Memory, the water of Mnemosyne... When you have absorbed it, your possession will be total, absolute, the occult Soul of the entire Masonry will have passed into you . The shock of this bitter taste awakens by impregnating him the memory of a past world, of a primordial unity of which only the memory remains in the forms acquired by the virtues that initiation offers him to practice ; every initiation aims to rediscover the memory of origins. This practice will bring him back to a more spiritual life, in which he will be led to climb a ladder of values other and much higher than that of simple secular existence. At every step, the recipient of the Eleusinian mysteries was threatened with Death and it was only by showing that he was always ready to undergo it that he reached the final revelations. One of the most terrible trials he had to endure was the following: Two glasses were placed in front of him. The high priest said to him: "Son of the Earth, one of these two glasses contains a terrible poison. If you really believe in the afterlife, if you're not afraid of dying, choose one of these glasses and drink. May the Gods protect you!" In case of refusal, the recipient was imprisoned until his death. The trials of initiation at different degrees were marked by absorption of beverage to be found in *Crata Repoa , or initiations into the ancient mysteries of the priests of Egypt* [45].

At ROPM, a third cup, containing milk, is offered to the new initiate, just before he carries out his first work on the raw stone, explaining to him that this beverage is " *both symbolic and sacramental, it will provide vitality to be reborn into your new life, because it is, like the blood which boiled in the Holy Grail, the igneous fermentation of life or of the generative mixture, the food of children and of the gods; and thereby the divine will be in you ." Sang Ra All* , "the ray comes from the cosmos", named *Gardal* on the banks of the Nile, it became *Gradal* ... then *Grail* . It was in this Gardal that the priests kept the material fire, as the priestesses kept the celestial fire of Ptah [footnote to the ROPM initiation ritual] .

Scottish General Grand Lodge (1804) and Réa	*Guide to Scottish Masons* (c. 1806-1811,	*Ritual of the first three degrees* according to

---

[45]Crata repoa or initiations into the ancient mysteries of the priests of EGYPT , 1821: <tinyurl.com/crata-repoa-mysteres-d-Espagne>.

Oiler of De Grasse-Tilly (1813)	published c. 1816-1821)	old notebooks (1829)
At the bottom of the steps of the altar, on a sacred cup. Drink a cup of water, then bitter water. *I commit to the most absolute silence on all types of tests to which my courage will be subjected; if I must false my Oath and fail in my duties, if the spirit of curiosity leads me here, I consent that the sweetness of this beverage changes into bitterness and that its salutary effect turns against me into subtle poison*	Kneeling at the bottom of the altar steps. Drink a little water from the sacred cup, then water with bitter . *I commit to the most absolute silence on all types of tests to which my courage will be subjected*	Kneeling at the foot of the altar. Drink a cup of sweet water, then a cup of bitter mixture. *I undertake on my honor to the most absolute silence on all types of tests to which my courage may be subjected.*

Let us recall that the new Prophet, that is to say the initiate in the seventh and last grade of the initiation of Egyptian priests, was presented with a drink called *Oimellas* (wine and honey), and he was told that he had reached the end of all the trials. There is reason to believe that the drink of a sweet and pleasant liquor that was presented to the new Prophet was an allegory which should mean that, from now on, he would only have the sweets of science to collect .[46]

In Anglo-Saxon rituals, there is no cutting of symbolic grades.

---

[46] p. 39 and Editor's Note M, p.50 *Crata Repoa, or Initiations to the mysteries of the priests of Egypt,* 1821: <tinyurl.com/crata-repoa-mysteres-d-Espagne>.

10 I DRANK WELL, I ATE WELL... AT THE BANQUET OF ORDER

Many traditions teach that the regeneration of fallen man occurs through the administration of food or drink, whether it is an elixir, communion or ambrosia. It seems that there is a physical and concrete transformation, caused by a food.

In Egyptian secret societies, the banquet marked the first degree of initiation. In the ancient Greek cults, and notably among the Pythagoreans, the sacred character of the banquet was so strong that the followers were only admitted to the meal after a period of three to five years after their entry into the Order.

Syssitie was a meal during which, in a ritual cup, the Greeks put a little flour, a little honey, and wine from Samos. After mixing well, they poured a spoonful of this mixture into the sacred fire, and thus offered the divinity a share of the sacred meal, then the cup was circulated among the celebrants. "Those who have invited the gods to their table," says Herodotus , will be invited, after death, to the eternal banquet in the islands of the Blessed."

In Plato's time, the banquet was in fact a meeting in two stages: first a meal, during which there was no drinking, which ended with a libation of pure wine, that is to say with the pouring on the ground of a part as an offering to the gods. Then came the symposium, properly the name of the banquet, marked by the moderation of the consumption of food and wine, a time devoted to exchanges. The most famous Banquet is the one described by Plato which would take place in 416 BCE [47].

In Freemasonry, in the 18th century, this practice of bounty in speculative Lodges was so common that it was customary to call Freemasons "Brothers of the Stomach". We also find as a mockery the expression "Knights of the stomach" [48].

In a letter from Laurence Dermott, added in 1764 to the 5th edition of the work entitled *The Constitution of Freemason, or Ahiman Rezon* [49,] we can read a philippic evoking the banquets of the *Moderns* : " We thought it appropriate to abolish the old usage to occupy themselves in the lodge with the study of geometry, and it seemed to some of the young Brothers that a good knife and a good fork in the hands of a skillful Brother, applied to suitable materials, would give greater satisfaction, and add to cheerfulness, than the strongest ladder and the best compass …".

---

[47] Video: < tinyurl.com/le-Banquet-de-Platon >.

[48] < tinyurl.com/exposition-franc-maonnerie >.

[49] Ahiman Rezon or help to all that are free and accepted masons… Paragraph XXX: <tinyurl.com/Ahiman-rezon>.

Inebriation , which was undoubtedly not lacking at these banquets , was often mentioned not only by laymen of the time, but also in the disclosures: " if the time does not allow us to carry out the instruction of the Lodge, … They take off their jewelry and they get drunk like Freemasons ." In 1720, in the words of Masonic songwriters we also find: "They make you a mason for 5 guineas, it's not much to pay, and then you can call the Lords and Dukes your brother, you have gloves, a white apron, you get drunk and that's it"

Of course, abuse was not uncommon; thus, William Hogarth's satirical engraving, entitled *The Night* , shows a Freemason leaving a tavern in a state that can be described as "charged" [50]. This figure is generally considered to be the Venerable of Hogart's lodge, Sir Thomas de Veil, supported by the guard of the Masonic lodge *(tyler)* , identified as Andrew Montgomerie, great wig maker . However, Philippe Langlet, in *Reading Images of Freemasonry,* thinks that it would rather be an innkeeper, given the candle-snuffing scissors which hangs on his apron (and not the key to the lodge).), as he was able to see in another engraving of an innkeeper wearing the same apron.

The fact that the first lodges met in taverns – after which they were named – can easily explain their bad reputation [51]. Thus, the name "À l'Oie et le Grill" the tavern of one of the 4 lodges which united into the Grand Lodge of London and Westminster, was a parody of the musical

---

[50]Engraving by William Hogarth: <tinyurl.com/Hogarth-la-nuit>.
[51]Lurker, *Banquet of Order at the French Rite* : <tinyurl.com/Banquet-d-ordre-au-RF>.

society the Swan and the Lyre of Apollo which had the habit of meeting in the same building before it was transformed into a tavern. But above all, as reported in the *New Catechism of Freemasons* in 1740: "It is because the Parisian lodges initially knew no other way of working than banquets, that they invariably met at restaurateurs . Among these, there were some who sought to exploit the situation, by being received as Masons and even by acquiring the right to keep a lodge. However, the Master of the Lodge who sold food and drink had a natural tendency to be primarily concerned with his commercial interests. Under his direction, Masonic work was in great danger of losing the character of dignity which befits it. This subsequently led to serious abuses. Certain lodges gave rise, in fact, to criticism which was unfortunately too justified . Any candidate was admitted, provided that he was able to cover the initiation costs; then, "chewing work" openly became the essential thing, Masonic Instruction concentrated with predilection on this grotesque and in no way initiatory vocabulary, which we sometimes persist in using in feasts or order banquets [52].

In response to detractors, Knight Andrew de Ramsay wrote in particular : " Our feasts are not what the profane world and the ignorant vulgar imagine. All vices of the heart and mind are banished and irreligion and libertinage, unbelief and debauchery have been proscribed. Our meals resemble those virtuous suppers of Horace where we discussed everything that could

---

[52]Oswald Wirth, *Freemasonry made intelligible to its followers* , 1923, p.12: <tinyurl.com/le-livre-de-l-apprenti>.

enlighten the mind, regulate the heart and inspire a taste for the true, the good and the beautiful .[53]
It seems that at this time when political parties and guilds were prohibited, the organization of banquets made it possible to get together around an authorized festive pretext [54]. "Most Assemblies of Freemasons are held at Caterers, or Wine Merchants. Sometimes the Reception takes place in a Bourgeoise house, and the meal at the Cabaret; the favorite Cabaret is the one whose Host; The Jacks are initiated into the Order, which they believe to be a shelter against the Police.

Articles 22 to 27 of the *General Regulations of Anderson's Constitutions* of 1738 refer to the organization of an annual banquet, as had already been provided for in Articles 22 to 30 of the *General Regulations* of 1720 [55]of the Grand Lodge of London and Westminster under the name of "feast". During post-revolutionary times, when Masonry was dormant, the banquet was a perfect way to meet.

What is beyond doubt is the permanence of the practice of feasting among masons, particularly as an element of reception [56]since, according to the royal ordinances

---

[53]Ramsay, Reading of a text initially scheduled for March 21, 1737: <academia.edu/34983131/>

[54] (p.101), *New catechism of the Freemasons* . 1440 since the Flood (1740): <tinyurl.com/nouveau-catechisme-des-fm>.

[55] *Constitution, histories, laws, charges, regulations and customs of the very venerable brotherhood of accepted Freemasons. *, p. 75: <tinyurl.com/usages-des-francs-macons>.

[56]G.-L. Pérau , *The Order of Freemasons betrayed and the secret of the Mopses revealed* , 1758, p. 69: <tinyurl.com/francs-macons-trahi>.

which regulated the profession, the reception of new masons had to be followed by a large meal. taken together [57] during which fraternal hugs were exchanged and the message of peace would be spread through bread and wine. However, there is an ambiguity in the text which could suggest that the ceremony took place during the banquet. Thus we read in Article 9 of the *Willam Schaw Statutes of* 1599, "It is ordained, by my Lord the Overseer General, that all the ancient statutes and regulations, established by the predecessors of the Masons of Kilwinning, be, future, faithfully observed by people in the trade, and that any apprentice or journeyman can henceforth only be received in the church of Kilwinning only, its parish and second lodge ; and that all reception banquets for apprentices or journeymen will be held in the said Lodge of Kilwinning" but especially article 11: " All apprentices to be received will only be so if they first pay for the aforesaid banquet the sum of six pounds, or else they will pay the banquet for all the members of the trade belonging to the said lodge and its apprentices .

It was not until the end of this century that the lodges began to be numbered. Previously, a Masonic lodge took its name from the inn, tavern pubs in London, back rooms of caterers in Paris, in which the brothers met.

The legendary meeting, which determined the birth of the Grand Lodge of London and Westminster (that of the English, the *Moderns*), would have been held on June 24, 1717 (or, according to the Julian calendar in force in England at the time, on June 4, 1717). July of the same

---

[57] < anciendevoirs.com/page-14 >.

year) in the tavern *At the Apple-Tree* (au Pommier), tavern on Charles-street, Covent-Garden. The four founding Lodges were, in addition to the one which accommodated 3 others, *At the Goose and Gridiron* , a brewery in St. Paul's Church-Yard, a five-story brick house with the dining room on the second floor, where the brothers met, measuring approximately 28 m2; *At the Crown* , brewery in Parker's Lane near Drury Lane; and *At the Rummer and Grape* (à la Coupe et au Raisin, Loge de Désaguliers), on Channel Row, Westminster. Then, officially, on St. John the Baptist's Day, the Assembly and Feast of Free and Accepted Masons was held at the aforementioned Goose and Grill in the courtyard of St. Paul's Cathedral. Before dinner, the eldest Master of the Lodge proposed a list of suitable candidates; the brothers, by majority and by show of hands, elected Anthony Sayer (member of *Antiquity Lodge No. 1* which still exists today), gentleman, Grand Master of Masons who was immediately invested with the decorations of his office by the most old Master, installed and congratulated by the assembly who paid him homage.

The report of this first meeting was written by James Anderson himself in 1738 and included in the 1784 edition. Roger Dachez says: "1717 is simply the historiographical myth, forged for "the right motive", which shaped forever the organization of all Freemasonry throughout the world. It's a a symbolic landmark in Masonic history and, as such, it will be celebrated around the world. That France, "eldest daughter of masonry", could be the only country where this would not happen would therefore be pure and simple absurdity [58].

In fact, what was founded on this solstice 1717, is nothing more and nothing less than a society of Taverns bringing together other clubs of the same order around the idea of organizing, together, a Saint's Day celebration. -Summer jeans, so that the festivities cost less for everyone. What remains very particular about this foundation is the appropriation to which it was subject.

To the extent that this grouping was made up of important scientific and cultural personalities, it was agreed to give it a name reminiscent of an already existing company with a good brand image, or even a tradition of protection and a certain freedom of action. Ancient masonry was therefore arbitrarily freed from its own duties and mysteries to become "free", *free* and it was called *freemasonry* .

As for the meeting which determined the collective existence of the *Grand Lodge* (that of the Irish, the *Ancients*), it was held on July 17, 1751 at the *Turk's Head Tavern* in the Greek street in the north London district of Soho, on the geographical opposite of the founding site of the Lodge of 1717 to the south. And in 1753, at St John's Winter (as opposed to St John's Summer where the Grand Lodge of London and Westminster was created), the Grand Lodge of Elders was created. *Turk's Head* Taverns And *Queen's Head* were very old and had long served as the headquarters of social societies, literary, philosophical and artistic clubs and circles. It was

---

[58] Roger Dachez, *The non-event of 1717* : <tinyurl.com/le-non-evenement>.

in one of these two taverns, the *Queen's Head* , that the Phylomusicae society met, the oldest source of a ritual practice of the rank of Master. This new structure then took the habit of meeting in a tavern occupied by an eighth Lodge which came to join them and offer them its premises; the " *Temple and Sun* " Lodge on Shire Lane in Temple Bar, another district of London.

In Paris, on June 12, 1725, the Saint Thomas Lodge, created at the instigation of Lord Derwentwater, a Jacobite Catholic refugee, set up in a tavern-caterer very frequented by English immigrants, at *Barnabé Hute* , rue de la boucherie. A competing Lodge was installed by Calvinist Protestants in 1732, a few streets further, at *the Auberge du Louis d'Argent* (it appears on the General Table of 129 workshops of 1930 under number 90) [59].

In 1737, Masonic meetings being prohibited by royal orders and decrees of Parliament, a police raid led by police commissioner Jean de Lespinay took place at the lodge located at the *caterer Chapelot* , rue de la Rapée![60]

The practice of Order Banquets is relatively little attested in the history of masonry, unlike that of simple banquets. A description of a banquet, then called "feast", accompanied by songs, is made by Louis Travenol in 1744 in chapter VIII, entitled *Ceremony of feasts and penalties*

---

[59] Plate no. 7a of the text Religious *ceremonies and customs of all the peoples of the world* <tinyurl.com/planche7coutumes-du-monde>.

[60] Religious *ceremonies and customs of all the peoples of the world* : <tinyurl.com/la-descente-de-police>.

for faults committed [61], of the disclosure *New Catechism or The Desolation of the Modern Entrepreneurs of the Temple of Jerusalem, or New Catechism of the Freemasons*

There are no real traces of banquets ordered by a specific ritual before the very beginning of the 19th century; this practice is only attested on the continent, more particularly in France.

The Emulation style outfits consist of a lodge ritual and an obligatory protocol banquet during which it is customary to deliver communications or boards which may be the subject of fraternal debates. It is also, in good practice, the time that the visiting Venerable Masters will choose to give their greetings and impressions. This banquet is the strict equivalent of the Chain of Union of continental rituals. Not participating means leaving the chain [62].

The Banquet of Order, or symbolic banquet, is a ritual meal, considered as an obligation, organized most often around the astronomical solstices, the winter solstice which announces renewal (on Saint John the Evangelist , December 27) but also that of summer when the sun approaches the zenith (on Saint John the Baptist, June 24). The shape of the tables is entirely astronomical; at the summer solstice, it represents the course of the sun in the upper hemisphere; at the winter solstice, that in the lower hemisphere. As a result, the Venerable, who

---

[61] Louis Travenol , *New catechism of the Freemasons, containing all the mysteries of masonry...* <tinyurl.com/ceremonie-des-festins>.

[62] Truthlurker searches and symbols, *Table Protocol:* < tinyurl.com/table-protocol>.

according to Masonic ritual represents the sun, occupying the extremity, or solstitial point, is always the highest point, in winter as in summer.

The room where the Order Banquet takes place must be located so that nothing can be seen from outside. The table is horseshoe-shaped, the officers occupy a specific place reminiscent of those inside the temple. The apprentices serve the food; the companions the wines. The candlesticks are placed on the table. A ribbon demarcates the center of the table along which the cannons (glasses) are aligned which, according to the French Philosophical Rite, must be "fire glasses", that is to say flat -bottomed glasses , and not glasses. stemmed glasses . _ [63]

The Order Banquet is an outfit that is done with bare hands, without an apron, only cords and necklaces are worn.

The works of table consist of seven health

It is in memory of ancient customs and traditional honors paid on the occasion of ritual meals that healths are worn. The 7 healths relate to the libations made by Persian, Egyptian and Greek initiates, in honor of the 7 planets, whose days of the week bear their names.

~The first libation was formerly offered to the Sun, king of the universe, to whom nature owes its fertility; it was dedicated to the sovereign.

---

[63] *French Philosophical Rite at the grade of Apprentice according to the original texts of the Respectable Loge Tolérance GODF , Paris 1950: <tinyurl.com/rite-francais-philosophique>.*

~The second libation was offered to the Moon, to this star which, according to the ancients, shed light on the most secret mysteries. The Masons dedicated it to the supreme power of the Order which, for them, is after the sovereign, the supreme regulator.

~The third was dedicated to Mars (Ares in Greece), a divinity who, among the ancients, also presided over councils and battles. The Masons made it the health of the Venerable.

~The fourth was that of Mercury to whom the Egyptians gave the name Anubis, the god who watches, the one who announces the opening or cessation of work. It has become the health of the Supervisors who announce, like Anubis, the opening and closing of the work, and who are responsible, like Mercury, for monitoring the brothers in the temple and outside the temple.

~The fifth was offered to Jupiter, also called Xenius the god of hospitality. It is dedicated to visitors and affiliated workshops, that is to say Masonic guests.

~The sixth was that of Venus, the goddess of generation; this divinity, symbol of nature, says Lucretius, is the charm of men and gods. It has become the health of the officers, that of the members of the lodge, that, above all, of the new initiates.

~Finally, the seventh libation was offered to Saturn, to this god of periods and times, whose immense orbit seems to embrace the entire world. It was chosen for the health of all the Masons who cover the surface of the Earth in whatever situation fate has placed them. Just as in the festivals of Saturn the slaves shared the pleasures of their Masters, and sat at their table ; Likewise among Masons, servants come to mingle in the work of the brothers (and sisters) to participate in this general health. We insert between the sixth and the seventh all those that we judge to add. The first three as well as the last are shot standing up [64].

Normally following the indications in the footnote of the *Precious Collection of Adonhiramite Masonry* , those to whom health is brought should never drink with others, but afterwards, as an act of thanks. We see that the apprentices ask to speak to express their recognition of the testimony of esteem and friendship they have received; they mark it by in turn carrying health [65].

To bring health, in most rites, the brothers (and sisters) stand up and place themselves in order at the table as it is said: "all the brothers will place their right hand flat on the table, their thumb in square. The apprentice brothers will place their towel (symbol of "to serve", "in the service of") on the left arm , folded squarely in front of the body. The companion brothers will wear it on the left shoulder . The Masters, rolled around their necks . The cup will be held in the left hand . It is therefore no longer the apron, but the napkin, placed in various places on the guests' bodies, which is the mark of the guest's rank.

---

[64]From page 35, see the chapter "Table or Banquet Lodge" in the *Guide to Scottish Masons or Notebooks of the three symbolic grades of the Ancient and Accepted Rit*: <reunir.free.fr/fm/rituels/guide>.

[65]Louis Guillemain Saint-Victor, Published in 1785, p.34: <tinyurl.com/recueil-precieux>.

It is with the towel that the Chain of Union is linked [66]. The most commonly practiced Chain of Union is the one with crossed napkins. Each participant holds, in the left hand, the left end of the napkin of his neighbor on the right and the right end of his own combined. The right hand remains free. If necessary , you can form a long chain without crossing the towels, with both hands occupied.

The table terms used during the Order Banquet are of military and alchemical inspiration. Here are some matches:
plate/tile; drink/fire a cannon; bottle/barrel;
chairs/stalls; cider or beer/yellow powder; knife/sword;
spoon/trowel; cut/trim; water/weak powder,
fork/pickaxe; fulminating liquor/powder; lights/stars;
eat/demolish materials; food/materials; tablecloth/veil;
bread/raw stone; dish/tray; yellow pepper/sand;
salt/white pepper; napkin/flag; table/platform;
glass/cannon; white wine/strong powder; red wine/red powder.

At the Forest Rite, the banquet is called Table Sale. This rite uses other table terms here is an overview: table/charcoal place, glasses/vans; bottles/masses; dishes and plates/plates; tablecloth and napkins/linen; spoons/shovels; forks/bows; knives/axes...

---

[66] Instructions in the table lodge as well as numerous information on this subject will be found in the document of the *French Philosophical Rite according to the original texts of the Respectable Lodge Tolerance* (1970-1985) starting on page 127: <en06.fr/wa_files /ritual%20rite%20french.pdf>

The table ceremonies of the High Grades, reported in the Thuileurs of the beginning of the 19th century, provide us with the outlines, such as for example Le *Manuel Masonnique Ou Tileur De Tous Les Rites De Maçonnerie Prâtiqués* , by Vuillaume, published in 1820. These banquets or table lodge have only few differences on some gestures, on the vocabulary [67]. Thus, in the 4th degree of the 1st order of the moderns , glasses are called urns and knives daggers. At the 18th degree of the REAA, the glasses are called chalice but there is a warning: banquets should not be confused with the mystical supper whose ceremonies are described in the rituals. Indeed, in the ritual of the eighteenth degree of the RÉAA, we find it specified that the reception of a newly consecrated Rosicrucian knight bears the name "supper".

Obviously, cheers change depending on the degree.

We also find these disclosures in the *Masonic Manual, or Tuileur of the Various Rites of Masonry practiced in France, in which we find the Etymology and Interpretation of the Names and Mysterious Words Given in each of the degrees of the different Rites* of 1830 with the description of banquets practiced in the High Grades: "There was, originally, what was called a refectory, where people only ate standing up, and where only vegetables cooked in the oven were served. water… When the space allows it, the table is given the shape of a Greek cross. The glasses are called chalices, the table is called the altar. The surplus of utensils has the same

---

[67]They can be consulted by leafing through pages 140, 166, in the *Masonic Manual Or Tiler of All Practical Masonry Rites* , 1820, by Vuillaume: <tinyurl.com/Tuileur-de-tous-les-rites>.

denomination as in the first degrees. Thus , we hear in the commandments for health: "Arise, knights! The saltire flag! Hand to the chalice! Up the chalice! It is raised to forehead height. Let's empty the chalice in three steps! The chalice on the left shoulder! The chalice on the right shoulder! Up the chalice! Let's put down the chalice! Mine for the drums! [68]".

Today, to evoke Masonic banquets, in the absence of respect for ritual forms, Freemasons speak of agape. Agape is an oblative love, that is to say giving priority to the needs of others over one's own. It is a love whose Latin equivalent is *Caritas* , different from those categorized by the Greeks, namely: carnal *Eros* , *Philia* for friendship and the pleasure of companionship, *Storgê* for family affection, *Ludos* λυδός playful love, *Mania* μανία obsessive love, Pragma πρ ᾶ γμα lasting love, Philautia φιλαυτία self-love.

Note that the acronym for "AGAPE", ἀ γάπη, brings together principles of the Christian religion and Stoic philosophy : *A* *gapè* amour; *G* *nothi* know yourself; *A* *necho* endures, endures; *P* *istuei:* to have faith, to have confidence; *E* *podos* take some distance, abstain.

---

[68] *Sublime chapter Bernard of Clairvaux, "The Last Supper of the Rosicrucian Knights",* from page 63: <fliphtml5.com/lxqr/xefi/basic>.

11 SKINNING: NEITHER NAKED NOR CLOTHED

Stripping of clothing, stripping of metals, stripping of speech and freedom of movement are metanoia widely practiced during Masonic initiation ceremonies. The Masonic stripping carried out during this initiation ceremony is a condition of separation from membership in a (profane) group in order to be able to be aggregated to another (sacred) group. Philippe Langlet gives us some valuable thoughts [69].

The stripping of metals is traditionally done in the forecourts, in the interval which separates the reflection room from the passage under the lower door. The preparers actually remove from the recipient all their metals without exception (money, coins, jewelry, etc.). Stripped of his metals, the Freemason renounces everything that connects him to earthly possessions as well as to profane merits. The stripping of metals is a moral renunciation enlightened by the assimilations of metals to the vices that Apollonius of Tyana made of them: silver with slavery, brass with pride, iron with envy or revenge. .

---

[69] <academia.edu/7620392/>.

must be experienced, in order to move from the condition of having to the state of being, from Baal to יהוה.

Raoul Berteaux, in his *Symbolic at the Apprentice Grade* , says: "Any metal carrier unknowingly picks up electromagnetic waves. He is at all times subject to influences which he does not perceive and, a fortiori, which he does not control. Freemasonry invites its members to renounce all their prejudices, habits and neuroses and in particular the powerful neurosis of the ego. It takes a look of courage to question yourself. This is not the complacency that the mirror offers. Becoming sensitive to one's daily life and wanting to consciously modify it by finding a tone of the heart is not simply a philosophical thought but a real spiritual work requiring an effort and an active will to sacrifice something, to renounce modalities of the self in order to to create another and act on the world. We see there a pact of narcissistic renunciation in exchange for total hope as Daniel Pons writes: "Creator, my brother, when you feel your ephemeral body abandoning you, then remember that the boat of Isis is a chariot which leads, towards eternity, all bodies exhausted by surpassing themselves".

There is also talk of abandonment of the old man.

In Anglo-Saxon masonry, the stripping of metals has fallen into disuse. The rite devotes a lot of care to the clothing preparation of the candidate, insisting very strongly on the fact that he must present himself to the Initiation *nor naked nor clad* , neither naked nor clothed, prepared in his heart. The Americans of THE emulation rite even force the recipient to undress completely and put on a sort of pajamas. But they speak neither of the four elements nor of the metals, with as much emphasis as Continental Masonry.

To strip oneself of one's tools for a companion is to free oneself from the supports which allowed the acquisition of the degree of knowledge which, if it had truly been acquired, would then be integrated into one's being. To be able to access a higher degree of order, "it would be appropriate for this knowledge of the companion to leave the way clear again and thereby to get rid of everything which has now become external to the being and which would hinder this next passage, even if these tools have been necessary until then.

In the Bible the serpent is presented in Genesis, 3,1 as "aroum" (עָרוֹם) cunning, but this word also has the translation "wise", "almost naked", "with torn clothes". This qualifier is found in Genesis; 3,7 to speak of the state in which Adam and Eve discover themselves (often translated as naked) and in Isaiah, 20, 2 associated with the word dislodged, iaheph (יָחֵף), state in which God commands Isaiah to put himself before prophesying, in short **neither naked neither dressed** !

Neither naked nor clothed

Man's first garment was his skin.
Egyptian priests , to sacrifice to the sun, laid down their rings and other gold or silver ornaments [70].

---

[70]Note 2, p. 46, *Masonic Manual or Tuileur of all Masonic rites practiced in France ,...,* 1820, by a veteran of masonry, believed

In most rites, neither naked nor clothed is the state in which the applicant is at the start of the initiation ceremony. In fact, the future initiate has his left arm and breast uncovered, in other words the heart uncovered as a sign of sincerity and frankness, right leg and knee exposed to mark the feelings of humility which must govern the pursuit of truth, foot left 'shoeless" (monoplaster) in imitation and memory of the ancient hero who limped in the darkness (Jason, the Argonaut, conquering the Golden Fleece).

In the Indian zone of influence, it is customary for Buddhist monks to keep their right arm bare. It is also a mark of humility, a sign of respect towards those present. Therefore, the disciple will take care to have his arm bared in front of his master(s). Furthermore, this bare arm shows that we are ready to work (a bit like here, we roll up our sleeves to get to work).

Albert G. Mackey uses the word "discalceation" to refer to the loosening of a foot [71]. This is the order given to Isaiah in Is, 20, 2 to put on "aroum" and "iaheph" (וְיָחֵף עָרוֹם), "in torn clothes" and "shoeless" before prophesying. In the Hebrew Bible, in the book of Joshua, it is written "take off your shoe from your feet, for you are entering a sacred place". We often think that this is perhaps the origin of this posture. But the

---

to be Claude-André Vuillaume: <tinyurl.com/Tuileur-de-tous-les-rites>.

[71] *The Symbolism of Freemasonry* , chap. XVIII, The Rite of Discalceation, 1882: <tinyurl.com/la-discaleation>.

meaning would be more to be sought in the Book of Ruth.

In some rituals (like Duncan's), the Candidate stands at the northeast corner and gives his left shoe to the Worshipful Master while the Bible verses of Boaz's purchase of Ruth are read: "a man tore off his shoe and gave to his neighbor; and this was a testimony in Israel; therefore the kinsman said to Boaz, Buy it for yourself. So he took off his shoe. Indeed, "formerly, in Israel, when it came to redemption or exchange, this was the procedure to make a contract final: one of the contracting parties took off his sandal and gave it to the other" (Ruth; 4, 4 to 9). Thus, at the York Rite, Brethren are called to testify that the recipient has entered Freemasonry and is in the process of ratifying his or her commitment to the Lodge. His shoe is then returned to him.

In the *Wilkinson Manuscript* of 1727 it is written: "Q: How were you made a Mason? A: Neither sitting, nor standing, nor naked, nor clothed, but according to the required forms. Q: What are the required forms? A: With the bare knee on the ground in the branches of the square and my left hand on the Bible, my right hand extended, with the compass on the bare left breast; [in this provision] I took on the solemn obligation of the Mason." We also find in the *Dialogue between Simon, a sedentary mason, and Philippe , a passing mason* [72], a reprise of the ritual of the new Freemasonry of the Grand Lodge of London and Westminster published in 1725: "Philip: How were you received as a mason? Simon: Neither

---

[72]p. 177: <tinyurl.com/harry-Carr-catechismes>.

naked, nor clothed, nor standing, nor lying, nor kneeling, nor standing, nor barefoot, nor shod, but in a ritual manner" (on December 12, 1728, the Ipswich Journal reported an "accident" of reception where the recipient fled into the street in the face of the attempt to put him in this symbolic outfit [73].

In The *Mason Unmasked or the True Secret of the Freemasons* of 1786, we find an explanation: "we uncover his left breast to represent the innocence of his heart, and the purity of his intentions. His left foot is put in a Slipper in allusion to what God said to Moses at the burning bush, take off the shoes from your feet, for the earth on which you walk is holy ground (Ex; 3,5).
His right knee is held bare, in memory of the "Calus" that St. John, Patron of the Order, had on his knees."

In the *apprentice catechism of the Precious Collection of Adonhiramite Masonry* (1785) we find another explanation: Q. Why did the Expert make you neither naked nor clothed? A. To prove to me that luxury is a vice which only imposes on the vulgar; & that the man who wants to be virtuous must put it above prejudice [74].

We can think that in the absence of a criminal record in the 18th century , the bare shoulder would have made it possible to verify that the future initiate was not marked with the fleur-de- lys , symbol of royal condemnation (not verified).

---

[73]Michel König, 1717-1747: The 30 glorious years of the Grand Loge des Modernes seen by the press of the time, Numérilivre.
[74]< tinyurl.com/usage-ni-nu-ni-vetu >.

More probably, the exposed throat undoubtedly made it possible to verify that it was not a woman who presented herself for initiation: "And the uncovered left breast tells you that as we do not admit any woman into our lodges, we let us fear being deceived by the disguise they could use to penetrate our mysteries [75].

Abuses of this practice have been noted in mixed lodges [76].

For Oscar Wirth: "The region of the heart is exposed by allusion to the absolute sincerity of the recipient; the nudity of the knee means that by bending it, it comes directly into contact with sacred ground, which it treads on its side, with the bare foot. Tradition reports that the knee is the seat of the body's strength, allowing standing and movement in perfect verticality, the prerogative of man which allows him to join the earth and the sky. If, moreover, we notice that the foot, the knee and the heart are placed in golden proportion, the primordial link with the seat of consciousness appears.

During his elevation of the Rite of Misraim, the companion **must be without shoes, his arms and breast bare, he must have a small square hanging from his right arm, a rope at his belt making three turns.**

---

[75]The order of Freemasons betrayed and the secret of the mopses... , 1758 , p. 53: <tinyurl.com/mamelle-decouverte>.
and page 45 of the Statutes and special regulations for the police of the Lodge...of the Count of Clairmont, 1768.
[76]The mason: <tinyurl.com/abus-en-mixite>.

In the rituals of the High Grades of Memphis Misraim, the adept will be clothed in cloaks of different colors; that of azure is both a protective barrier against attacks from outside and the shell of a psychic egg where the initiate withdraws into himself, receives cosmic waves and causes the spiritual harvest to germinate within him. The tradition of the cloak is Hellenic and Pythagorean, it is the classic garment of the philosopher.

Half-naked, half-dressed would be a good expression because if the applicant must abandon the old man, he nonetheless remains himself, not like an infant, but like a consciousness organized by his profane life, with which makes him a unique person and constitutes him as other. Half-naked to be able to put on a new myth, half-dressed to be a solid stone to help build the temple. Half-naked, half-clothed removes the uncertainty of neither naked nor clothed.
In the sense of half-naked, half-dressed, we can see, upon leaving the reflection room, that the profane clothes of the applicant have been torn as in the germination of a seed, the germination of a new being whose clothes are assimilated to his "skin" which will become light; in Hebrew the words skin, âur (עור) and light, aur (אור) are similar...

This stripping of the recipient is in accordance with many initiatory traditions which begin with a renunciation, a stripping, we then say abandon the old man.

Once "peeled," the recipient becomes a pilgrim.

12 THANKING IS NOT ALWAYS SAYING THANK YOU

When a brother (or sister) thanks in the box, he is often echoed by this sentence: "we don't thank you in the Lodge !" .

Surprising in a society where courtesy[77] is considered a virtue [78]. The philosopher André Comte-Sponville even makes it the mother of virtues [79].

However, the terms *thank / thank you* appear clearly in the Masonic rituals of the [18th] century :
- Published in 1785, the *Precious Collection of Adonhiramite Masonry* specifies: those whose health one bears must never drink with others, but afterwards, **as an act of**

---

[77]Polite attitude recognizing the generosity of others through a thank you.

[78] Dante affirms that at this age [of companion] the fundamental task that must be accomplished consists of seeking one's own perfection, and in this regard he considers it necessary to develop five virtues: temperance, strength, fraternity , courtesy and loyalty.

[79]From 19'38: <tinyurl.com/Comte-Sponville-spiritualites >.

thanks . We see that the apprentices ask to speak to express their recognition of the testimony of esteem and friendship they have received; they mark it by in turn carrying health [80].

- Bazot's *Freemason's Manual* (1817) mentions giving thanks in the lodge [81].

So where can this assertion "we don't thank in the Lodge" come from, which is surprising to say the least?

Several hypotheses are proposed:

1) "In many states, when a professional Companion had finished his tour of France and he wanted to settle in any place, **he thanked his Society** , that is to say he left. withdrew with a certificate, delivered to him in a large meeting, by his colleagues, a certificate attesting to the morality and wise conduct of the person who obtains it: this certificate is a **kind of leave** . The person who has given thanks no longer belongs to the active Society, he no longer owes anything to it, he is independent. However, he remains attached to this Society at heart and loves it as a good soldier loves his regiment and his old comrades in arms, with whom he suffered and fought for a long time; he even loves him to a greater degree, because his attachment was always free and only lasted as long as he wanted: also this Society could still

---

[80] Louis Guillemain Saint-Victor, *Recueil precious de la masonry adonhiramite,* 1785, p.34: <tinyurl.com/Recueil-precieux-FM>.

[81] At the 3rd and 5th health of the order banquet, p. 192: <tinyurl.com/Manuel-du-franc-macon>.

on a great occasion count on his pecuniary assistance and on his person.[82]

"We never thank in a Lodge", could then take the meaning that having been initiated creates an emotional and supportive bond between brothers and sisters *which does not change, even when leaving Freemasonry.* Reality challenges this hypothesis!

2) However, there are companies where we never thanked people in this sense for leave; that of the Companions foreign stonecutters is of this number! It was Perdiguier who informed us about this detail.

Hence a second explanation: " **The** *fellow stonecutters , of whom we are the heirs, were not in the habit of thanking. We must comply with this usage.*"

This same semantic shift in this explanation is no more satisfactory since it is not appropriate: "you don't thank people in the box" is a remark made precisely to those who are in the box!

3) " **In a progressive and socializing vision** , the fight against the powerful and **for social emancipation** led to the idea that acts as simple as the request for apology or thanks were the infallible mark of the homage that the weak – or the "oppressed" – were doing by obligation to the dominant elites – the "oppressors"! The Freemason, at the forefront of the social struggle, had to **renounce these manifestations of servility** . In this new

---

[82]Agricol Pertiguier, *The book of companionship*, T1, 1857, p.69-70: <tinyurl.com/le-lvre-du-compagnonnage>.

intellectual atmosphere, the principle of the fundamental equality of all the Brothers gradually imposed the idea that they owed each other neither excuses nor thanks… [83]" In Portuguese, merci is said " *obligo* " and reflects this well. of this vision of the relationship induced by a thank you. Taken to the extreme, it could be understood as "putting oneself at the mercy" of another.

However, thank you is also a testimony of recognition. Should Freemasons be ungrateful because of traces of the practices of operative Freemasons or because of a hint of class struggle?

How can we be satisfied with these explanations since saying thank you is also an "obligation" of decorum between equals [84] (showing that we feel obliged to have received, **thank you being a way of giving reciprocally**), a politeness, one of the "the tender things of life". So would it be inappropriate to show a word of gratitude for what we have received as a share, the work of a board for example, by a thank you?

A priori, in the secular world, this would be the least of things. But here it is: listening to a board happens during an outfit with a very ritualistic characteristic.

---

[83] Roger Dachez, *We do not thank in Freemasonry - and we do not apologize either:* <tinyurl.com/on-ne-s-excuse-pas>.

[84] Agricol Pertiguier, *The companion book* , T1, 1857, p. 237: Languedoc - **You have many kindnesses** for me, Pays Provençal, and for all this **I can only help you thank** : <tinyurl.com/dialogue-compagnons>.

particular . The speaker addresses everyone present, not in particular to the one who would like to thank. *The floor is given to everyone.* So wouldn't thanking mean appropriating the indivisible totality of what is offered and showing egotism?

How can we not deprive the brother (or sister) who has worked hard of the pleasure/salary he would experience from receiving this "sweetness of life". The **Venerable alone** could he not do it, **thanking in the name of all brothers and sisters present** ? It would be appropriate for him to do this for each board, whatever its quality, **in order to suspend any judgment** . In other words, **it would be appropriate for it to be a phrase of the ritual** and not expressions of affection or appreciation which can always be done afterwards in a damp room. And it is just as much in the name of all the brothers and sisters that the Venerable **thanks the visitors** because they come to help with the work on the site.

Praying Hands is a drawing by Albecht Dürer to thank his brother Albert for having financed his studies while the latter was dying in the mine [85].

I'll let you listen to Sinéad O'Connor
In *Thank You For Hearing Me* .[86]

---

[85] Executed around 1508, Albertina Museum, Vienna
[86] Sinéad O'Connor, *Thank You For Hearing Me:* <tinyurl.com/merci-de-m-avoir-ecoutee>.

ABOUT THE AUTHOR

Jacques-André editor
TU, *Letters of Passion,* 2001 (Laure de Noves Prize)

EDITIONS of La Hutte
To light the way, A philosophical approach to Freemasonry , 2011
Vocabulary of the Apprentice Freemason , 2nd [edition], 2012
Vocabulary of the Freemason Companion , 2012
Master Freemason Vocabulary , 2013
Drawing elements with ruler and compass, The Masonic Concordance , 2015
What does it mean to cut your stone ?, 2015

EDITIONS ledifice.net
Gathering what is scattered , 2020
Vocabulary of the Apprentice Freemason , 3rd [edition], 2020
Vocabulary of the Freemason Companion , 2nd [edition], 2021

Ubik EDITIONS
Once upon a time, Hiram , 2021
Masonic gestures , 2021

Numérilivre EDITIONS _
Masonic traces, the spirit of geometry , 2022

Dervy EDITIONS
Vagabond Dictionary of Masonic Thought , 2017 (**literary prize of the Masonic Institute of France** , Essays and Symbolism category)
Freemason. How to move from profane to sacred , 2023

www.ingramcontent.com/pod-product-compliance
Lightning Source LLC
Chambersburg PA
CBHW012308240726
48656CB00008B/2595